Moving to Ireland
A Practical Guide

C L Mitchell

www.relocatingtoireland.com

Disclaimer

Although the author has made every effort to ensure that the information in this book was correct at press time, the author and publisher do not assume and hereby disclaim any liability to any party for any loss, damage, or disruption caused by errors or omissions, whether such errors or omissions result from negligence, accident, or any other cause.
Unless specifically stated, the reference to any company, organisation, product or book does not constitute and endorsement or recommendation.

ISBN-13: 978-1533240835
ISBN-10: 1533240833

DEDICATION

This book is dedicated to my loving husband. I would not have achieved this book without his love and support.

Contents

1 MOVING

Practical and Essential Information

Capital City: Dublin

Provinces and Counties: There are four provinces in Ireland – Connacht, Leinster, Munster and Ulster. There was once a fifth province called Meath, but it was incorporated into Leinster and Ulster. These provinces contain 32 traditional counties, six of which are located in Northern Ireland.

- *Connacht:* Galway, Leitrim, Mayo, Roscommon, and Sligo.
- *Leinster:* Carlow, Dublin, Kildare, Kilkenny, Laois, Longford, Louth, Meath, Offaly, Westmeath, Wexford and Wicklow.
- *Munster:* Clare, Cork, Kerry, Limerick, Tipperary, and Waterford.
- *Ulster:* Antrim, Cavan, Donegal, and Monaghan are located in the Republic of Ireland, while Armagh, Down, Fermanagh, Londonderry ("Londonderry" is generally preferred by unionists and "Derry" by nationalists), and Tyrone are Northern Ireland.

Population: Over 4.5 million.

Language: English. Irish is the official language but it is only spoken in the Gaeltacht communities along the west coast.

Currency: Euro (€).

Time Zone: GMT+1 (GMT+1 March to October).

Ireland Phone Code: +353

International Access Code: 00

Emergency Services (Police, Fire, Ambulance): In Ireland both phone numbers 999 and 112 exist equally and run in parallel. Regardless of which number you call in Ireland, it will be handled in the same manner by emergency services.

Police Services: In Ireland, the Police services are referred to as the *Gardai* or "the guards". An individual officer is called a *garda* (plural *gardaí*), or, informally, a "guard". A police station is called a *Garda station*. The Gardai do not carry firearms.

Voltage: 230V/50hz

Visa requirements: Most citizens of Europe, Australia, New Zealand, USA and Canada are visa exempt. All countries not on the visa exempt or the Irish Short Stay Visa Waiver Program list need a full passport as well as a short stay 'C' visa in order to visit Ireland. This short visit visa is valid for a maximum of 90 days.

Embassies and Consulates in Ireland: For a full list of the foreign embassies and consulates in Ireland, refer to Ireland's Department of Foreign Affairs website *dfa.ie*.

Refugee Support in Ireland: Refugee's can access support and advice through the Irish Refugee Council *irishrefugeecouncil.ie* and Refugee Legal Services through the Legal Aid Board *legalaidboard.ie*.

Vaccinations: There are no required vaccinations for travelling to Ireland.

Seasons: The traditional Irish seasons are:
- *Spring:* February to April
- *Summer*: May to July
- *Autumn*: August to October
- *Winter*: November to January

However, Met Éireann, Ireland's Met Office, has the seasons occurring one month later than these traditional seasons.

Weather: Ireland's weather is influenced by the Atlantic Ocean and consequently does not experience the extreme temperatures of other countries at similar latitudes. Irish weather is unpredictable and changeable, however, it never usually gets too extreme. The warm ocean current called the North Atlantic Drift keeps sea temperatures relatively mild and the coastal hills and mountains protect the island from strong winds coming off the ocean.
The temperature in Ireland is measured in Celsius (0°C is equal to 32°F). Spring temperatures range from about 4 to 20°C; summer 8 to 26°C; autumn 9 to 25°C; and winter 4 to 14°C.

Measurements: Ireland uses the metric system. This means that liquids are measured in millilitres and litres, weight is measured in grams and kilograms, and distance and road speed signs are displayed in kilometres. Since 2005 all new cars sold in Ireland have speedometers that display only kilometres per hour. However, people still like to measure themselves in stones, and bars still use "pint of beer".

Driving: Ireland drive on the left hand side of the road.

Postcodes: Ireland rolled out postcodes in 2015. To find a post code visit Eircodes website *finder.eircode.ie*.

Holidays: Ireland has nine public holidays. Employees generally receive four weeks of annual holidays per year.

Tipping: There is generally no tipping culture in Ireland.

Value Added Tax: Value Added Tax is charged at different rates for various goods and services. You can get an extensive list of VAT ratings from Ireland's Revenue Commissioners website *revenue.ie*.

- 23% is the standard rate of VAT on all goods and services (unless a reduced rate applies as below).
- 13.5% is a reduced rate of VAT for items including fuel (coal, heating oil, gas), electricity, veterinary fees, building and building services, agricultural, contracting services, short-term car hire, cleaning and maintenance services.
- 9% is a special reduced rate of VAT for tourism-related activities including restaurants, hotels, cinemas, hairdressing and newspapers.
- 4.8% is a reduced rate of VAT specifically for agriculture.
- 0% VAT rating includes all exports, tea, coffee, milk, bread, books, children's clothes and shoes, oral medicine for humans and animals, vegetable seeds and fruit trees, fertilisers, large animal feed, disability aids such as wheelchairs, crutches and hearing aids.

LGBT: Ireland is a pretty tolerant place for gays and lesbians. Bigger cities such as Dublin, Galway and Cork have well-established gay scenes. In 2015, Ireland overwhelmingly backed same-sex marriage in a historic referendum. However, you'll still find pockets of homophobia throughout the island, particularly in smaller towns and rural areas.

Resources:
- *gaire.com* has a message board and information for a host of gay-related issues.
- LGBT Ireland's website *lgbt.ie* provides support and information (including social) and advice.

Disability: All new buildings have wheelchair access and many hotels have installed lifts, ramps and other facilities. However, there are many old buildings in Ireland and many of these are not easily accessible to people with a disability. Fáilte Ireland and

NITB's accommodation guides indicate which places are wheelchair accessible.

In big cities, most buses have low-floor access and priority space on board and these are becoming more available on regional routes. Trains are accessible with help. In theory, if you call ahead, an employee of Irish Rail (Iarnród Éireann) will arrange to accompany you to the train. Newer trains have audio and visual information systems for visually impaired and hearing impaired passengers.

Resources:
- Ireland's Citizen Information website *citizensinformation.ie*.
- Legless in Dublin website *leglessindublin.com* is a great resource for those using wheelchairs and living / visiting Dublin.

Vegan, Vegetarian, Coeliac & Gluten Intolerant: It is becoming much more common place for restaurants in Ireland to provide food options for the various dietary requirements. However, Ireland's love of meat can make it difficult for vegetarians and vegans. The Vegan Society of Ireland website *vegan.ie* and The Vegetarian Society of Ireland website *vegetarian.ie* provide useful information about where to shop and eat whilst living in Ireland.

Although the Irish have a high incidence of coeliac disease, there is a general lack of understanding of the dietary needs. The Coeliac Society of Ireland website *coeliac-ireland.com* provides information and support for people living in Ireland who eat gluten free. They also contain a list of gluten free products available at the supermarkets in Ireland.

Drinking Laws: In an attempt to curb alcohol problems, Ireland has a number of strict alcohol laws in place.
- The legal age to buy alcohol in Ireland is 18 years of age. You must be able to prove your age using a passport, National Identity Card, Garda Síochána Age Card (Age Card issued by Irish Police), or drivers licence.

- Since August 2003 it is illegal in Ireland to sell alcohol at reduced prices for a limited period during any day. In other words, 'happy hour' is prohibited.
- Pub closing time midweek is 11.30pm with a half hour drinking up time. Friday and Saturday nights is 12.30am with a half hour drinking up time.
- Most nightclubs that have a full bar will serve drinks until about 2.30am.
- Off-licence sale of alcohol is only permitted between the hours of 10.30am and 10.00pm on weekdays and 12.30pm to 10.00pm on Sundays or St Patrick's Day. Sales are not permitted on Good Friday or Christmas Day.
- Every pub shuts on Good Friday and Christmas Day. Alcohol cannot be purchased anywhere on these days.
- It is an offence for you to be drunk in a public place, however this is largely overlooked if you behave yourself.

Planning Your Move to Ireland

The decision to relocate to another country can be difficult. This section aims to assist you through the decision making process by outlining the considerations that need to be made and provides an overview of what moving to Ireland entails.

Deciding Whether to Make the Move

Moving to another country is not only stressful and daunting, but also expensive. If you are planning to move to Ireland as a family group, then take the time to discuss it as a family. Make sure that everyone gets the time to air their concerns.

Before committing to the move, consider renting a holiday home in your location of preference and stay for as long as possible. Use the opportunity to connect with people in your job industry to see whether there are any job opportunities that would be available to you. Take note of the cost of living and go to the local pub and talk to the locals to find out more about the community. Particularly in smaller Irish communities, the locals can be very friendly and enjoy chatting to visitors.

But remember, holidaying in Ireland is a lot different than actually living here. Even if you decide to relocate to Ireland, it may not be feasible for you to do so with the strict immigration laws. Unless you have been offered a job with a company that will assist you to obtain a work permit, then you may find it difficult to gain the necessary permission to relocate and work in Ireland.

You also need to consider the actual cost of the move. Don't underestimate the cost of relocating to another country. Even if you have a job lined up, unless your new employer is willing to foot the bill for your moving expenses, then you are going to need a significant sum of money just to cover the initial moving costs.

For example:

- *Immigration costs*: Work permits are not cheap. You may also need to renew your passport if it does not have enough time left on it.
- *Moving costs*: The cost of relocating all of your belongings can easily run into thousands of dollars. To reduce costs, try to bring as little as possible as many homes in Ireland are rented furnished.
- *Plane tickets:* Costs vary depending on time of year, how far you book ahead and the distance that you are travelling. If you are planning to bring pets over, then this can be a significant additional cost.
- *Health Insurance:* If you are not eligible for Irish public healthcare, then you will need to purchase Irish private health insurance before you arrive.
- *Initial short term accommodation when you arrive:* Depending on what part of Ireland you are planning on relocating to, short term accommodation can be very expensive, especially in Dublin.
- *Rental deposit and advance:* If you are planning on living in rented property, then you will need to pay an upfront rental deposit as well as a months rent in advance.
- *Setting up home:* All those little things that you will need to purchase when you get to Ireland like a linens, food stores, really add up.

- *Furnishing your new home*: Consider the cost of furnishing your new home versus the cost of bringing your furniture with you.
- *Purchasing a new car*: Owning and running a car in Ireland can be expensive. Depending on where you live, you may be able to rely on public transport and postpone this cost, or you may even decide that you don't need one at all.
- *The cost of selling your home:* If you currently own a home, then consider the costs associated with selling it. How strong is your real estate market? Alternately, consider renting it out. Then, if it doesn't work out in Ireland at least you will have will have avoided these additional costs and still have somewhere to live when you return.

Getting to Ireland

Flights

Ireland has three international airports which are located in Dublin, Cork and Shannon. It will depend on where you are flying out of as to which airport options you will have available to you. Dublin is Ireland's main airport, but the other airports also provide a number of flights to a range of destinations throughout the EU and EEA.

- Cork Airport *corkairport.com*
- Donegal Airport *donegalairport.ie*
- Dublin Airport *dublinairport.com*
- Ireland West Airport Knock *irelandwestairport.com*
- Kerry Airport *kerryairport.ie*
- Shannon Airport *shannonairport.ie*

Ferries

You can get a ferry to either the Republic of Ireland or Northern Ireland. Ferries are a popular choice for those coming from Europe and wanting to bring their car. There are a number of ferry companies that operate services to Ireland from Europe.

Irish ferries depart from:
- Fishguard, Holyhead and Pembroke, Wales
- Liverpool, England
- Roscoff and Cherbourg, France
- Cairnryan and Troon Scotland
- Douglas, Isle of Man

Moving Companies

Moving your personal effects to Ireland will not be cheap. Moving companies typically charge by volume. If you only have a small amount of items to ship then it may be cheaper to transport your items in a shared shipping container. If you have a lot of items, then it may be more cost effective to pay for an entire shipping container.

If you only have a small number of boxes to move, you may find it difficult to source a company willing to take on such a small job. But don't give up. Keep ringing around the companies and you will eventually find someone that will ship your goods. Prices vary wildly, so it's worthwhile taking the time to get a number of quotes.

Be aware that if you pack yourself, some moving companies won't pay for breakages. If that's the case, then you may be better off paying for the company to pack them for you. Also, if access to your current or new home is difficult, you may be charged more.

Be prepared to wait a long time for your shipped items to arrive in Ireland. When I moved from Australia, it took four months for mine to arrive! Depending on where your items are being shipped from, they may need to go through UK customs before being transported into Ireland. This can extend the shipping time.

Packing

When packing, make three piles – 'definitely taking with me', 'definitely getting rid of' and the 'maybe' pile. If you have the time to begin sorting your belongings early, try packing up the 'maybe' items and putting them away for a while. Then, when you go through the 'maybe' items again closer to your moving date, it's easier to make a final decision. Ask yourself, did you honestly miss any of it? If not, then do you really need to take it with you?

When it comes to your electrical goods you need to consider your options. You can get cheap adapter plugs in Ireland for about €2 from the bargain stores. You could also get the plug on your power cord changed. However, standard voltage in Ireland is 230V AC, so if your electrical goods don't run on this voltage you will need to get converters for them.

If you are planning to take a fridge freezer with you, make sure that you allow enough time for it to be defrosted. Do not pack perishables like food, plants and flammable items.

Make sure any clothing or bedding packed is clean. If items are left dirty for a length of time, then they can form yellowy brown oxidation stains that are extremely difficult to remove. If this does happen to you, then try scrubbing the stains with any of these items:

- Soft soap (handwash)
- Washing detergent
- Shampoo
- Lemon juice
- Oxygen bleach made into a paste

After treating with one or more of these options (sometimes on tough stains I've been know to try all of them), soak the items in a diluted bucket of oxygen bleach. *Don't* be tempted to use chlorine bleach on these types of stains as it will just set the stain and then you will never get it out.

Selling Your Unwanted Items

Selling your unwanted stuff takes a lot of work and is time consuming. Take photos of each item and set a price. However, you will need to be flexible with the price if you want to get rid of things quickly.

Sell items of value online using Ebay, Gumtree etc... You can also try selling your items by posting or emailing the list through your work, your kid's schools, and on community notice boards. Try and include lots of photos from different angles and measurements.

Schedule time to hold a garage sale. Make sure you well advertise it via social media, local community sites and even putting signs out. On the day, make sure you lock up your house, secure valuables, and have someone to help you keep an eye on things. If you don't like the idea of holding a garage sale, then take your items to a local car boot sale or flea market.

Important Documents

Scan or take photo's of all of your important documents and save them onto your own personal storage device and the cloud, e.g. Dropbox account, to ensure they don't get lost.

Take this opportunity to scan all of your non-digital photos. It's actually very cheap to get this done professionally. That way, if the originals get lost at least you have a copy of them.

It's safer to transport your most important documents with you in your carry on luggage to reduce the risk of them being stolen or lost. It also makes them easily accessible if you need them as you go through Irish immigration when you arrive in Ireland.

For example:
- Birth and marriage certificates.
- Insurance policies.
- Passport and immigration documents such as your visa and work permits.
- Your new employment contract.
- Employment records.
- Academic record and certificates.
- Medical documents such as vaccinations, medical, dental and optical records.
- Property documents.
- Living will and testament.
- Bank account details and recent statements.

Moving Checklist

Set up a moving calendar to help you stay organised and on track for a successful move.

6 to 12 Months Before Departure

- Set up a moving calendar. If moving with family, post your calendar somewhere that everyone can see it.
- Start a relocation budget spreadsheet. Begin with a predicted budget using estimated costs and then add in your actual costs as you go.
- Plan when you are going to quit your current job. Consider the required notice periods in your employment contract.
- Commence immigration applications and obtain / renew your passport if required.

6 Months Before Departure

- Research for potential job opportunities and update your resume and LinkedIn profile.
- Research and contact potential schools / child care.
- Once your immigration visa and work permits have been approved, book your flights.
- Commence the process for relocating your pets.
- Book your moving company.
- Book temporary accommodation in Ireland.
- Notify your children's school / day care that you will be moving and arrange for any relevant information to be transferred.
- Arrange to collect medical, dental, prescription / medications, vaccinations records.
- Scan or take photos of important documents and non digital photos. Store them to a memory device as well as the cloud, e.g. Dropbox account.
- Begin sorting items and selling / giving away what you don't want.
- Begin packing items that you won't need before you move.
- If you have access to good cheap medical care, consider getting a check up at your doctor, dentist, and optician. This will allow you to resolve any potential medical issues so they don't get in the way of your move.
- If you are planning on renting out your current home, then set up meetings with prospective property managers and get

your property valued. Get feedback on any improvements that need to be done to the property to gain maximum rental returns. Schedule time to either do it yourself, or book someone else to do it for you.

2 Months Before Departure

- If you are selling your furniture (beds, fridge etc...) then consider either borrowing or hiring essential items to use up until your departure so you can sell your own items in advance.
- Depending on your work contract, resign from your existing job providing the required notice period. You are going to need a good reference from your employer when you begin looking for work in Ireland, so leave on good footing.
- Obtain financial and tax statements.
- Arrange to pay outstanding bills.
- Schedule time to farewell friends and family.
- Continue to sell unwanted items online.
- For smaller items, or those that haven't sold online, schedule a garage sale or sell at items at a car boot sale.
- Arrange travel insurance.
- Arrange for Irish Health insurance.
- Cancel the gas, electricity, oil, internet, phone, and mobile phone (you may want to keep your mobile phone connection until you arrive in Ireland. Once there, you can purchase a prepay Sim card until you are able to make other arrangements. Just make sure that your phone is set up for roaming services so that it still works outside of your home country.)
- If you are planning to rent your home, then arrange the necessary insurances e.g. landlords insurance as well as rental property insurance. Remember to schedule your existing household insurance to end when the new insurance arrangements take over.
- Set up direct debit for any bill payments that need to occur while you're away.

- Set up online banking and online access to any other accounts that you will need to keep open. Arrange to receive statements online to avoid issues with them getting lost in the mail.
- Fill any medication scripts that you will need.
- Arrange for regular deliveries to be cancelled prior to you departing e.g. newspaper, milk, magazine subscriptions etc…
- Claim unused points on club cards or points schemes and then cancel them if no longer needed.
- Go through all the food in your pantry and begin eating your way through it.

1 Month Before Departure

- Buy some Euro so that you have local currency when you arrive.
- Notify your Bank and arrange for cash / travellers cheques / travel debit cards. You need to ensure that you have access to enough cash when you arrive in Ireland as you may initially have difficulty opening a bank account.
- Get rid of unsold items via charity shops and freecycle websites (where you can offer your goods for free). At least it will go to someone who will reuse it, instead of the landfill.
- If you have arranged to rent your house out, then make sure that you arrange to have the household bills that they will be managing redirected to them, e.g. council rates, landlords insurance etc… Also, decide whether you will be doing the final property clean yourself or hiring someone to do it for you. Your real estate agent should have a qualified company they work with that they can recommend.
- Notify change of address with anything that requires it.
- Consider getting a redirect to your new address. If you don't initially have one, consider getting it redirected to a trusted family member or friend that you feel comfortable with opening your mail for you. They can send on any important documents via email or post.

- Finish packing and make an inventory for the moving company (also required by customs).
- Finalise what you will be taking with you in your suitcases. Consider the changes in season that may occur while you are waiting for your goods to be shipped.

Tips

- If you love online shopping, then don't forget to change your delivery address in your account settings.

2 RELOCATING WITH PETS

Moving to Ireland with Pets

Pets are valued members of our family and it's important they come with us when we relocate. But there are a number of important steps that you must take in order to get your pets to Ireland safely and smoothly. Below is a detailed guide on what is required to move your pets to Ireland based on the type of pet you have and whether you are coming from an EU or non-EU country. Be aware that some airlines in some countries may require you to use a professional pet relocation service which will increase the cost of their trip. But do shop around, as quotes can vary greatly.

Important

- The movement of live animals to and from Ireland is regulated by Ireland's Department of Agriculture, Fisheries and Food *agriculture.gov.ie*.
- Snub nosed / short nosed dog and cat breeds are more prone to respiratory problems during air travel. Consult with your vet before transporting a snub nosed animal.
- Although no dog breeds are banned in Ireland, there are restrictions on certain dog breeds. Refer to the section 'Pet ownership in Ireland'.

Moving Pets into Ireland from the EU

Cats, Dogs or Ferrets

Your pets may enter any Irish port of entry including airport and ferry terminals.

Your pet must:
- Be identified by a microchip*.
- Have an EU passport which certifies that the animal is immunized against rabies. In addition, dogs from Finland, Malta and the UK must have been treated against Echinococcus multilocularis (tapeworm) not more than 120 hours (5 days) and not less than 24 hours (1 day) prior to their scheduled arrival in Ireland.
- If you are moving more than five pets, they need to have a veterinary certificate as evidence that the animals have had a clinical examination within 48 hours of departing. However, if you can provide proof that your pets have been brought in to compete in a competition, then you will be exempt from this requirement.

Tips

- Pet passports are issued by Veterinarians.
- Refer to the list of EU ferry operators and airlines that will carry pets into Ireland from the EU on Ireland's Department of Agriculture, Fisheries and Food website *agriculture.gov.ie*.

Pet Birds^

- Pet birds may only be brought into Ireland when the owner is relocating or holidaying to Ireland.
- An 'Advance Notice of Import' form must be completed and submitted at least 24hrs in advance of the bird arriving in Ireland.
- The bird must travel either with its owner or the owner's representative and an 'Owner Declaration for Pet Birds'.

Pet Rodents and Rabbits

- The pet must travel either with its owner or the owner's representative.
- An 'Advanced Notice of Import' must be completed and submitted at least 24hrs in advance of the rodent or rabbit arriving in Ireland.

Moving Pets into Ireland from 'Low-Risk' Non-EU Countries

Cats, Dogs or Ferrets

Pets being transported into Ireland from a non-EU low-risk country can be brought in under the following conditions:

- Be transported in an approved airline / pet cargo carrier. Refer to the list of approved airlines / cargo handlers on the website *agriculture.gov.ie*.
- Enter Ireland only via Dublin Airport.
- Identified by a microchip*.
- Accompanied by a veterinary health certificate, Annex IV to Commission Implementing Decision 577/2013 certifying that the animal is immunized against rabies.
- Dogs must be treated against Echinococcus multilocularis (tapeworm) not more than 120 hours (5 days) and not less than 24 hours (1 day) prior to their scheduled arrival in Ireland.
- Have evidence that the pet is being moved for non-commercial purposes. This must be presented to the approved airline in advance.
- Be accompanying you on holiday or moving to Ireland. You must not be intending to sell your pet.

Pet Birds^

You must complete the application form for an 'Import Permit' within sufficient time to enable the pre-export requirements to be completed.

The bird must:
- Travel either with its owner or the owner's representative.
- Be transported in an approved airline / pet cargo carrier. Refer to the list of approved airlines / cargo handlers on *agriculture.gov.ie*.
- Be individually identified.
- Be accompanied by a veterinary health certificate signed by an official veterinarian to confirm compliance with the pre-export requirements.
- Be accompanied by a declaration signed by the owner / person representing the owner in the form contained at Annex 111 to in Commission Decision 2007/25/EC as amended.
- Be imported through either Dublin Airport or Shannon Airport.

Pet Rodents and Rabbits

- If you wish to import your rodent or rabbit, you need to complete and submit an application form for an 'Import Permit' as well as an 'Advance Notice of Import'. The application should be made in sufficient time to enable the pre-export requirements to be completed.
- The pet must be accompanied with a licence issued by the Animal Health and Welfare Division of the Department. The licence will set out the requirements for import which include a veterinary health certificate.
- The rodent or rabbit must be transported in an approved airline / pet cargo carrier. Refer to the list of approved airlines / cargo handlers on *agriculture.gov.ie*.
- For a non-domestic rodent or rabbit being kept as a pet, the owner is responsible for checking with the Parks and Wildlife section of the Department of the Environment as to whether a CITES licence is required to import such an animal.

Moving Pets from 'High-Risk' Non-EU Countries

Cats, Dogs or Ferrets

If your country is not on the non-EU low risk country list then you can only bring your pets into Ireland under the following strict conditions:

- Be transported in an approved airline / pet cargo carrier. Refer to the list of approved airlines / cargo handlers on *agriculture.gov.ie*.
- Enter Ireland only via Dublin Airport.
- Identified by a microchip*.
- Accompanied by a veterinary health certificate, Annex IV to Commission Implementing Decision 577/2013 certifying that the animal is immunized against rabies. Dogs must be treated against Echinococcus multilocularis (tapeworm) not more than 120 hours (5 days) and not less than 24 hours (1 day) prior to their scheduled arrival in Ireland.
- Undergone a blood test at least 30 days after rabies vaccination to confirm a neutralising antibody titration at least equal to 0.5IU/ml. Your pet may only enter Ireland when at least three months has expired since a successful blood-test.
- Have evidence that it is being moved for non - commercial purposes. This must be presented to the approved airline in advance (air ticket reservation etc...).
- Be accompanying you on holiday or moving to Ireland. You must not be intending to sell your pet.

Pet Birds^

You must complete and submit the application form for an 'Import Permit' within sufficient time to enable to pre-export requirements to be completed.

The bird must:

- Travel either with its owner or the owner's representative.
- Be transported in an approved airline / pet cargo carrier. Refer to the list of approved airlines / cargo handlers on *agriculture.gov.ie*.
- Be individually identified.

- Be accompanied by a veterinary health certificate signed by an official veterinarian to confirm compliance with the pre-export requirements and a declaration signed by the owner / person representing the owner in the form contained at Annex 111 to in Commission Decision 2007/25/EC as amended.
- Be imported through either Dublin Airport or Shannon Airport.

Pet Rodents and Rabbits

- The pet must be accompanied with a licence issued by the Animal Health and Welfare Division of the Department. The licence will set out the requirements for import which include a veterinary health certificate.
- The rodent or rabbit must be transported in an approved airline / pet cargo carrier. Refer to the list of approved airlines / cargo handlers on *agriculture.gov.ie*.
- If you wish to import your rodent or rabbit, you need to complete and submit an application form for an 'Import Permit' as well as an 'Advance Notice of Import'. The application should be made in sufficient time to enable the pre-export requirements to be completed.
- For a non-domestic rodent or rabbit being kept as a pet, the owner is responsible for checking with the Parks and Wildlife section of the Department of the Environment as to whether a CITES licence is required to import such an animal.

* European Pet Microchipping

The microchip must be a transponder readable by a device compatible with ISO standard 11785. If your pet has a different type of microchip, your vet can remove it and replace it with an EU compatible chip.

Tips

- Don't forget to update your personal contact details contained on the chip when you relocate.

Pet Birds^

Pet birds are defined as any species except fowl, turkeys, guinea fowl, ducks, geese, quails, pigeons, partridges and ratites reared or kept in captivity for breeding, the production of meat or eggs for consumption, or for restocking supplies of game. They must not be traded commercially.

Travelling with a Recognised Assistance Dog

These rules apply similarly to those travelling with the aid of assistance dogs. If the dog is accompanying a person from outside the EU, it is advised that they contact Animal Health Section of the Department of Agriculture, Food and the Marine (DAFM) before travelling:

- By phone: +353-1-6072827 or
- By email: pets@agriculture.gov.ie

Quarantine Requirements

If you are fully compliant with the regulations, then your pet will not need to be quarantined. Compliance checks will be carried out within approximately three hours of your pet arriving. Once these checks have been carried out, your pet will be released to you.

Important

If you do not comply with the regulations, then your pet will either be:

- Returned to the country it came from at your expense or
- Placed into quarantine for the necessary length of time for the animal to meet the health requirements. This is done at the expense of the owner.

The Sedation of Animals for Air Travel

Although animals may be excitable on the way to the airport and prior to loading, research has shown that they usually revert to a resting state in their dark, closed cargo hold and subsequently sedatives may have an excessive effect. Pets travelling by air frequently need veterinary care to recover from the effects of sedation and unfortunately many pets have even died from over sedation.

Some animals can react abnormally from sedation. In addition, the physiological changes from sedatives may be enhanced due to the air pressure inside the aircraft. Increased altitude can also create respiratory and cardiovascular problems for dogs and cats that are sedated or tranquilized. Pug or snub nosed dogs and cats are especially affected.

Sedation can also affect an animal's natural ability to maintain their balance and equilibrium. When the travel container is moved, a sedated animal may not be able to brace and prevent injury.

The Alternative to Sedating Your Pets for Air Travel

Veterinarians suggest pre-conditioning your pet to its travel container instead of sedating. You should do this as far in advance of your trip as possible.

Let your pet get to know the travel container that you will be using by leaving it open with a treat or familiar object inside e.g. a favourite toy. This will encourage your pet to spend time in it. Your aim is to make your pet as relaxed as possible in the container so that their trip is more comfortable.

Alternatives to Flying Your Pet in the Hold

If you are concerned about cost, or your pets ability to cope with a long flight in the hold, there are some alternatives to consider. For small pets, some airlines such as Air France will allow you to transport them in the cabin. This can actually work out cheaper than flying them in the hold.

An alternative to flying your pet is to travel on a boat which provides a kennel service. This may require you to travel to another part of the EU before travelling on to Ireland. This option of course takes much longer than flying, but combines the practicalities of travel with an enjoyable holiday. It's is also a great option for people who don't like to fly. Although your pet will be required to stay in the ships kennel, you can visit them during your journey. Most ships also provide a dog walking area. Be aware that due to size, some breeds cannot be accommodated. Your carrier of choice will be able to provide you more detail on their restrictions.

When arriving in the EU, you will need to satisfy the requirements of the country that you are entering. Be aware that some countries may ban certain breeds that they consider 'dangerous'. Consequently, boats entering these countries will not allow these breeds on board.

Arriving in Ireland with Pets

There are a number of accommodation providers in Ireland that allow pets, but some of them may charge an additional fee to accommodate them. There are also many that don't allow pets, so make sure that you book well in advance and make it clear how many pets you will be bringing, their breed and size so there is no misunderstanding when you turn up.

Pet Ownership

Once your pets have finally arrived in Ireland, the next step is understanding the Irish pet essentials. Like, what sort of pet insurance is available? And where can your pets stay while you're on holiday?

Cat and Dog Vaccinations

Vaccinating your pets is essential to their health and protect them from very contagious fatal diseases.

Your vet will provide you with a record of vaccination, showing the vaccines that have been administered to your pet and the dates that their next booster is due. This is an important document so keep it safe.

Dog Vaccinations

Dogs are vaccinated against distemper, hepatitis, parvovirus, leptospirosis, and kennel cough. Puppies should be vaccinated at 6-9 weeks of age and then again at 10-12 weeks. They will become fully protected two weeks after their second vaccination. Regular 'booster' vaccinations are necessary to keep your dog's immunity levels high enough to protect them against disease throughout their life. Your vet will advise you on how often your pet needs to be vaccinated.

Cat Vaccinations

Cats are vaccinated against feline infectious enteritis (FIE), cat flu, leukaemia virus (FeLV), and chlamydophilosis. Generally, kittens begin vaccinations at 9-10 weeks of age. They will need another vaccination at 12 weeks old. Most kitten vaccines are given as part of a series of injections to stimulate optimum immune response. Thereafter booster vaccinations at regular intervals, as recommended by your vet, are strongly advised to ensure continuing immunity.

Dog Ownership Regulations

In Ireland local authorities are responsible for dog control and they have the power to seize dogs, impose fines and take court proceedings against owners.

If your dog injures people or livestock then you will be liable.

Dog Licensing

If your dog is going to be staying in Ireland for more than 30 days then it will need to be licensed. To get your dog licensed, visit your local An Post office. Guide dogs are exempt from being licensed.

Dog Identification

Your dog must wear a collar that details its name and address. If you do not comply with this regulation, you may be given an on the spot fine.

From September 2015, the government introduced compulsory microchipping. If you are planning to relocate your dog to Ireland then this is a mandatory requirement for all dogs entering Ireland.

Dangerous Dogs

When in public, alongside the regulations outlined, the following breeds of dogs must be muzzled on a two metre leash and be led and controlled by a person over 16 years of age:

- American pit bull terrier
- English bull terrier
- Staffordshire bull terrier
- Bull mastiff
- Doberman pinscher
- German shepherd (Alsatian)
- Rhodesian ridgeback
- Rottweiler
- Japanese akita
- Japanese tosa
- Bandog

Dog Fouling

Many areas in Ireland suffer from considerable dog fouling. This problem is caused by apathetic dog owners and the common Irish practice of letting dogs (illegally) roam free. Don't be surprised to see a well placed dog turd sitting at the foot of a 'No dog fouling' sign! There are spot fines that are supposed to be handed out, however, it is a common issue raised in the local news that this regulation is not regularly enforced.

Pet Insurance

Unfortunately there is no public healthcare for animals. When your beloved pet becomes ill or gets injured, you may be faced with veterinary bills that can run into the thousands of euro's. Most of us don't have this kind of money lying around. Pet insurance provides a way of budgeting your pet's healthcare to enable you to afford the quality treatment they need and deserve.

There are a huge range of pet insurance providers to choose from in Ireland:

- Allianz *allianz.ie*
- Pet Insure *petinsure.ie*
- Pet Insurance *petinsurance.ie*
- 123 *123.ie*
- Quote Devil *quotedevil.ie*
- Insure 4 less *insure4less.ie*
- Blue Insurance *blueinsurance.ie*

- Sheridan *sheridan.ie*

Pet Insurance Terminology

Before you start comparing policies, here are some helpful tips and hints to help you understand pet insurance.

Premium

The amount that you pay for your insurance cover. Typically, the more expensive the premium, the more cover that you will receive. However, read the small print as you may end up unnecessarily paying for benefits that you do not need.

Policy Excess

The amount that you pay have to pay each time you make a claim. The excess may be a fixed amount per condition, or a fixed amount plus a percentage of the fees, or just a percentage of the fees. When choosing a policy, you will typically pay a lower premium by accepting a higher policy excess. As pets grow older, many pet insurance companies ask owners to pay a higher policy excess.

Third Party Cover

Many pet insurance companies offer third party liability cover for damage caused by your pet for which you may be legally liable.

Policy Exclusions

Policy exclusions are items that will not be covered by the pet insurance policy. Common exclusions include:
- Preventive or optional aspects of pet care e.g. vaccinations, neutering and parasite control.
- Pregnancy and whelping / kittening.
- Behavioural problems.
- Illnesses that start in the first 2 – 4 weeks of the policy's commencement date.
- Home visits by the vet.
- Pre-existing conditions (vets are often asked to submit details of pets' previous clinical histories to check for

these).

- Working dogs and dogs restricted under the Dangerous Dogs Act.
- Routine dental treatments.
- Special nutrition, such as 'prescription diets'.
- Travelling overseas.
- Complementary treatments, such as hydrotherapy, homoeopathy and acupuncture.
- Euthanasia and cremation.

Types of Pet Insurance Policies

Lifelong Cover

This cover is the most comprehensive but typically the most expensive. The policy is renewed annually, but any health conditions that your pet has developed during the year continue to be covered for the life of the pet.

Annual Cover

This cover tends to be less expensive, but it is likely to pay out less over your pet's lifetime. This policy is renewed annually, and only covers a condition for 12 months from its onset. However, after 12 months any condition claimed in the previous year is excluded from the insurance cover.

This type of cover usually provides insurance for one-off accidents or illnesses where your pet is treated and recovers. However, if your pet develops a long term chronic illnesses, the cover may not be enough.

Other Benefits

As well as cover for accidents and illnesses, some insurance companies may provide the following benefits:

- *Boarding kennel or cattery fees:* Covers the cost of boarding your pet if you are unable to care for your pet due to being hospitalised from illness or accident.
- *Holiday cancellation:* Any travel and accommodation expenses you cannot recover if you have to cancel your holiday because your pet is injured or becomes ill. Or, if

you have to cut your holiday short due your pet going missing or becoming injured or ill.

- *Advertising and rewards:* The cost of advertising if your pet is stolen or goes missing and the reward you have offered (amount must be agreed with your insurance company).
- *Third party liability and legal costs:* If property is damaged, or someone is killed, injured or falls ill as a result of an incident involving your pet.
- *Death from illness or accident:* Covers the price that you paid for your pet if it dies or has to be put to sleep because of an illness or accident.
- *Theft or straying:* Covers the price that you paid for your pet if it is stolen or goes missing and does not return.

What Happens to the Policy as the Pet Grows Older?

Many pet insurance companies have an age threshold beyond which they will not accept a new policy. But as long as your pet has been insured prior to this age threshold, most companies will continue to offer coverage.

However, when this age threshold is reached, you can expect the policy premium and excess to increase. The list of exclusions also typically gets longer, so carefully check your policy conditions when you are renewing it.

Tips

- Some insurance policies only cover for illness or injury, not accidents. So if you want your pet covered for accidents, check the policy details.
- Are you covered for emergency after hours care? After hours care is expensive, so if you want your pet covered for this service, check the policy details.
- Some pet insurance companies offer discounts for purchasing online.
- Some companies may provide a discount for old aged pensioners.

Animals on Irish Public Transport

Guide dogs and assistance dogs are permitted to travel on all services free of charge without restriction. Be aware that these service dogs must be wearing their official coat, medallion and lead to identify them as a working dog.

Pets on Irish Buses and Trams

Animals are not allowed on buses and trams (unless of course they are a service dog), however, don't be surprised if you occasionally see this happen. I have on occasion seen small animals snuck onto trams and buses. It is usually at the driver's discretion.

Pets on Irish Rail Services

The Irish Rail (Iarnród Éireann) service is much more flexible.

- Small dogs may be carried free of charge in the passenger compartment, but they must travel on the owners lap. Unless the dog is in the animal container, it must be kept on a lead at all times.
- Cats may be carried free of charge in the passenger compartment, but they must travel in a secure carrier on the owner's lap.
- Dogs and/or pets in containers found to be occupying a seat are liable to a penalty charge.
- Animals are not allowed in restaurant cars (with the exception of service dogs).
- If a customer objects to the presence of a dog in their carriage, the owner will be requested to move to another part of the train.

If your dog is not a small lap dog, it can still be transported on the Intercity services in a Guards Van (non-passenger compartment) if it is available (not all routes have this compartment available). Charges will apply.

Dogs conveyed in a Guard's Van must be:
- Secured with a collar and chain and muzzled.

- The container must be sufficiently large enough to allow the dog to stand up and lie down with ease and comfort and be adequately ventilated.
- All dogs must be properly labelled giving the name, address, and destination of the owner.
- Learn more about travelling with pets on the Irish Rail website *irishrail.ie*.

Pets in Taxis

Taxis are usually ok about transporting pets as long as they are in a container or you have them restrained and ensure that they sit on a blanket. However, it is at the driver's discretion as to whether they will take you.

Holidaying in Ireland with Pets

There are a number of accommodation providers in Ireland that allow pets. Some of them may charge an additional fee to accommodate them. But there are also many that don't allow pets, so make sure that you book well in advance and make it clear how many pets you will be bringing, their breed and size so there is no misunderstanding when you turn up.

Tips

- Can't take your pet with you while on holiday? There are lots of quality catteries and boarding kennels in Ireland. Find a boarding service near you by visiting the Irish Boarding Kennels and Cattery Association website *ibkca.ie* to get a listing of the services in your area

3 IMMIGRATION

Disclaimer: *Official policy and legislation regarding immigration continually changes. This information is meant to be used as a guide only. Please refer to the Irish Immigration and Naturalisation website inis.gov.ie for the latest and most up to date information.*

Unless you are an EU/EEA citizen then the Irish immigration process can be time consuming and frustrating. Please be aware that this is only meant to be used as a guide. You can access free immigration legal advice through the voluntary organisation FLAC. The FLAC website *flac.ie* provides details of their telephone and referral services, Legal Advice Centres, and online legal information.

Refugees

Refugee's arriving in Ireland can access support and advice through the Irish Refugee Council *irishrefugeecouncil.ie* and Refugee Legal Services through the Legal Aid Board *legalaidboard.ie*.

Short Stay Visas

EU/EEA/Swiss Nationals

Visitors from these countries (including British dependent territories) do not need a visa to visit Ireland and can enter using either their passport or their national identity card.

Irish Short Stay Visa Waiver Program

Under this program, citizens of holders of certain categories of Short Stay 'C' UK visas can travel to Ireland within the time remaining on their current leave to remain in the UK without the requirement to obtain an Irish visa.

The countries included in the Program are:

- **Eastern Europe:** Belarus, Bosnia and Herzegovina, Montenegro, Russian Federation, Serbia, Turkey and Ukraine.
- **Middle East:** Bahrain, Kuwait, Oman, Qatar, Saudi Arabia and the United Arab Emirates.
- **Asia:** India, Kazakhstan, Peoples Republic of China (excluding Chinese nationals of the Special Administrative Regions of Hong Kong and Macau), Thailand, Uzbekistan.

Visa Exempt Countries

To find out if you need to apply for a visa to visit Ireland, refer to the list of visa exempt countries on the Irish Citizens Information website *citizensinformation.ie*.

Non-Visa Exempt Countries

All other citizens from countries not on the 'Irish visa exempt list' or the 'Irish Short Stay Visa Waiver Program list' will need a full passport as well as a short stay 'C' visa to visit Ireland. This short visit visa is valid for a maximum of 90 days and you can apply for either a single entry or a multiple entry short stay 'C' visa.

Applying for a Short Stay Visa

To obtain an Irish short stay visa, you need to apply to the Irish embassy or consulate in your country of permanent residence. You may be required to attend an interview. If there is no Irish embassy or consulate in your country of residence then you may apply to any Irish embassy or consulate, or directly to the Visa Office in Dublin.

Tips

- To find for more information about short stay visas, visit the Irish Naturalisation and Immigration Service website *inis.gov.ie*.

Student Visas

EU/EEA and Swiss National Students

EU/EEA and Swiss nationals are free to study in Ireland and there are no special requirements. You do not need to register with the immigration authorities.

Non EU/EEA and Swiss National Students

Non EU/EEA and Swiss nationals must gain a place in an Irish educational institution in order to come and study in Ireland. Please be aware that you cannot move to Ireland to do a part-time or distance learning course. However, you can come to Ireland to undertake a short term English language course.

Students from Visa Exempt Countries

To find out if you need to apply for a visa to visit Ireland, refer to the list of visa exempt countries on the Irish Citizens Information website *citizensinformation.ie*.

Your passport will need to be valid for at least six months after the completion of your course. In addition, all non-EU/EEA students must register with the local Garda National Immigration Bureau.

Students from Non-Visa Exempt Countries

Students from countries requiring a visa to enter Ireland must apply for a student visa. When you arrive in Ireland you must also register with the local Garda National Immigration Bureau.

Applying for a Student Visa

You must apply for your student visa online using the AVATS online facility *visas.inis.gov.ie*. The application will only be processed once the online form is completed and the required documentation, passport photograph, and appropriate fee are received by the relevant office.

As part of the application process you will need to demonstrate that you have access to €7,000 to support yourself financially during your stay. You will need to have a letter from your course provider (e.g. college or university) confirming that you have been accepted and evidence that the course fees have been paid in full. Your passport will also need to be valid for at least six months after the completion of your course.

Student Permission to Work

Non-EU/EEA students are not entitled to Irish social welfare. However, those with a Stamp 2 are permitted to work up to 20 hours a week during term time. During the holiday periods May to August and from 15th December to 15th January, you can work up to 40 hours per week.

Students with stamp 2A permission are not permitted to work.

Non EU/EEA Students Arriving in Ireland

All non-EU/EEA citizens, whether visa-required or not, are subject to ordinary immigration controls when they arrive in the country. Although you may have successfully obtained a visa (or be exempt from needing one), you may still be refused entry by Irish immigration officials when you arrive. When arriving in Ireland you should show your acceptance letter from your school, college, or university to the immigration officer so that you receive the correct immigration permission stamp in your passport.

Please note:
- The Immigration Officer makes the decision on who is actually allowed to enter Ireland.
- They will stamp your passport for either one or three months.
- This means that you must register with the Garda National Immigration Bureau within the time limit stamped on the passport if you plan to stay longer.
- To ensure that you have no difficulties, it is recommended that you have your documents ready to show the

immigration officer when you arrive in Ireland.

Registering with the Garda National Immigration Bureau

Non EU/EEA students need to register at the Garda National Immigration Bureau (GNIB). In order to register, you need to visit your local immigration registration office and ask for the registration officer as soon as possible following your arrival in Ireland. Refer to the Garda *garda.ie* website to find your closest GNIB.

You will need to provide the following information:
- Valid passport (and entry visa if applicable).
- Valid Student card.
- Evidence of financial support.

Students from visa exempt countries: If you plan to stay less than six months, then you must demonstrate that you have access to €500 per month to support yourself during your stay. If you plan to stay longer than six months, then the requirement is €3,000.

Students from countries that are required to have a student visa: You must demonstrate:
- That you have access to €7,000 to support yourself during your stay.
- Evidence of private medical health insurance.
- A credit / debit card for payment of €300 fee.

The registration officer may also take your fingerprints, signature, and photo and may ask for further details.

On successful completion of your GNIB registration you will be issued with a GNIB Card. This is valid for one year or for single semester students, to the end of their course. Your GNIB card is valid for one year (unless you are a single semester student). It must be renewed each year by the expiry date.

Work Permits

EU/EEA/Swiss Nationals

EU/EEA/Swiss Nationals have the right to stay in Ireland with their family members for up to three months. However, if you plan to stay more than three months, you must either:

- Be engaged in economic activity (employed or self employed) *or*
- Have sufficient resources and sickness insurance to ensure that you do not become a burden on the social services of Ireland, *or*
- Be enrolled as a student or vocational trainee, *or*
- Be a family member of a Union citizen in one of the previous categories

You do not need an Irish employment permit or residence card to live here and are entitled to be treated the same as Irish workers.

Learn more about the residence rights of EU/EEA nationals in Ireland at the *citizensinformation.ie* website.

UK Citizens

Are entitled to live and work in Ireland without any conditions or restrictions and are entitled to be treated the same as Irish workers.

Other Countries

If you are from outside the EU/EEA or Switzerland then you need a permit in order to live and work in Ireland. These can be very difficult to obtain depending on your circumstances. When you apply for a work permit, you will be required to pay a fee.

General Employment Permit (formerly work permit)

These permits are available for occupations with an annual salary of €30,000 or more. Only in exceptional cases will jobs earning less than this be considered. Normally, a labour market needs test is required.

Critical Skills Employment Permit (formerly Green Card permit)

This permit is available for most occupations with an annual salary of over €60,000. They are also available for occupations on the Highly Skilled Occupations List that pay an annual salary of at least €30,000. There is no requirement for a labour market needs test.

Dependant / Partner / Spouse Employment Permit

This permit applies to spouses, recognised partners, civil partners and dependants of holders of Critical Skills Employment Permits or researchers under a hosting agreement. There is no requirement for a labour market needs test.

Reactivation Employment Permit

Allows foreign nationals who entered the State on a valid employment permit but who fell out of the system through no fault of their own, or have been badly treated or exploited in the workplace, to work again. Applicants for a Reactivation Employment Permit must first apply to the Irish Naturalisation and Immigration Service (INIS) for a temporary immigration permission Stamp 1. You can find the eligibility criteria, guidelines and application form on the website *inis.gov.ie*.

Contract for Services Employment Permit

For foreigners undertaking work with a contract to provide services to an Irish entity. These permits allow the transfer of non-EEA employees to work on an Irish contract in Ireland while remaining on an employment contract outside the State. Generally, a labour market needs test is required.

Intra-Company Transfer Employment Permit

Allows senior management, key personnel and trainees working in an overseas branch of a multinational company to transfer to the Irish branch. They must be earning at least €40,000 a year (trainees must be earning at least €30,000 a year) and have been working for the company for a minimum of 12 months.

Internship Employment Permit

Available to non-EEA national full-time students who are enrolled in a third-level institution outside Ireland and have a work experience job offer in the State.

Sport and Cultural Employment Permit

For employment in the State for the development, operation and capacity of sporting and cultural activities.

Exchange Agreement Employment Permit

For those employed in the State under prescribed agreements, e.g. the Fulbright Program for researchers and academics.

Working Holiday Maker Program in Ireland

Citizens of Argentina, Australia, Canada, Hong Kong, USA, Japan, New Zealand, South Korea and Taiwan may apply for a Working Holiday visa as part of a reciprocal agreement between these countries and Ireland. You also need to have sufficient funds to support yourself while looking for work. As a non-EU national, you must register with the Garda National Immigration Bureau. There is a fee of €300 for the issue of a Garda registration card.

US Work & Travel Program in Ireland

US citizens can enter Ireland on a Work and Travel visa, but they must either be in post-secondary education or have graduated within the last 12 months.

In addition, they will need to:
- Present an original bank statement showing that they have access to €1500 and a return ticket *or* access to €3000.
- Medical / travel insurance.
- Paid the relevant fee.

Students Working in Ireland

Non-EU/EEA students are not entitled to Irish social welfare, but those with a Stamp 2 are allowed to work up to 20 hours per week during term time. During the holiday periods May to August and from 15th December to 15th January, you can work up to 40 hours a week.

Students with Stamp 2A permission are not allowed to work.

Arriving in Ireland with a Work Permit

All non-EU/EEA citizens, whether visa-required or not, are subject to ordinary immigration controls when they arrive in the country. Although you may have successfully obtained a work permit, you can still be refused entry by the Irish immigration officials when you arrive. Make sure that you have all of your documents ready and easily accessible as you go through immigration. As well as your work permit, you should also have all of the documents that you submitted as part of your permit application.

Please note:
- The Immigration Officer decides who is allowed to enter Ireland.
- They will stamp your passport for either one or three months. This means that you must register with the Garda National Immigration Bureau within the time limit stamped on the passport if you plan to stay longer.

Registering with the Garda National Immigration Bureau (GNIB)

In order to register, you need to visit your local immigration registration office and ask for the registration officer as soon as possible following your arrival in Ireland. Refer to the Garda *garda.ie* website to find your closest GNIB.

You will need to provide the following information:
- Your passport.
- Your nationality, how and when you acquired it and your

40

previous nationality (if any).
- Date and place of your birth e.g. your birth certificate.
- Your profession or occupation.
- Documentation supporting your residence permission, e.g. your work permit.
- Your Irish employment contract.
- Your Irish address.
- The address where you last lived outside the State.
- A credit / debit card for payment of €300 fee.

The registration officer may also take your fingerprints, signature, and photo and may ask for further details.

On successful completion of your GNIB registration you will be issued with a GNIB Card.

Retiring to Ireland

Irish Citizens

Irish citizens returning to Ireland have an automatic right to reside here.

UK Citizens

UK citizens may live in Ireland without any conditions or restrictions.

EEA and Swiss Nationals

Can remain in Ireland with your family for up to three months without restriction. But if you are retired and plan to stay more than three months, you need sufficient resources and sickness insurance to ensure that you do not become a burden on the State.

Other Countries

If you are not from a visa exempt country, then you will need to obtain a visa to get into Ireland. Once you arrive in Ireland, you must obtain permission to remain by registering with your local

Garda National Immigration Bureau and prove that you have sufficient resources and health insurance to support yourself to ensure that you do not become a burden on the State.

Since March 2015, the Ireland Naturalisation and Immigration Service (INIS) changed the standards by which non-EU retirees are determined to be financially suitable for residency. The new rule requires that retirees have an annual income of no less than €50,000 per person, (€100,000 for a married couple) for the remainder of their lives in Ireland, regardless of their existing cash on hand or lack of debt.

Retirees have also had their immigration status changed from Stamp 3 to Stamp 0, which, according to the INIS website is "a low level immigration status which is not intended to be reckonable for Long Term Residence or Citizenship. It is granted to persons who have been approved by INIS for a limited and specific stay in Ireland."

Arriving in Ireland to Retire

All non-EU/EEA citizens, whether visa-required or not, are subject to ordinary immigration controls when they arrive in the country. Although you may have successfully obtained a visa (or not even need one), you can still be refused entry by Irish immigration officials when you arrive.

Please note:
- The Immigration Officer decides who is allowed to enter Ireland.
- They will stamp your passport for either one or three months. This means that you must register with the Garda National Immigration Bureau within the time limit stamped on the passport if you plan to stay longer.

To ensure you have no difficulties, it's recommended that you have your documents ready to show to the officer.

Registering with the Garda National Immigration Bureau

In order to register, you need to visit your local immigration registration office and ask for the registration officer as soon as possible following your arrival in Ireland. Refer to the Garda *garda.ie* website to find your closest GNIB.

You will need to provide the following information:

- Your passport.
- Your nationality, how and when you acquired it and your previous nationality (if any).
- Date and place of your birth e.g. your birth certificate.
- Documentation supporting your residence permission, e.g. visa if required.
- Proof that you have sufficient resources and health insurance to support yourself to ensure that you do not become a burden on the State.
- Your Irish address.
- The address where you last lived outside the State.
- A credit / debit card for payment of €300 fee.
- The registration officer may also take your fingerprints, signature, and photo and may ask for further details.
- On successful completion of your GNIB registration you will be issued with a GNIB Card.

4 HEALTHCARE

The Irish Healthcare System

There are two tiers of health services in Ireland:
- The Irish Public Health system
- The Irish Private Health system

The Irish Public Healthcare system is governed by the Health Service Executive (HSE) *hse.ie*. It provides health and social services to EU/EEA or Swiss nationals and residents of Ireland. In order to receive publicly funded health services, you do not need to be paying Irish tax or into social insurance, but you must be able to satisfy the HSE that you are 'ordinarily resident'.

To establish whether you are ordinarily resident, you must be able to demonstrate that you intend to remain in Ireland for a minimum of one year. As well as this, the HSE may request evidence, e.g.
- Proof of property purchase or rental, including evidence that the property in question is the person's principal residence.
- Evidence of transfer of funds, bank accounts, pensions etc…
- A residence permit or visa.
- A work permit or visa, statements from employers etc.
- A signed affidavit by the applicant.

If you do not come under one of these categories, then you can still receive healthcare but you will be charged the full cost of the service.

Unfortunately there are long waitlists in place for medical treatments, and, as a result, many people choose to take out private health insurance in order to receive medical treatments more promptly. In some cases where specialised treatment cannot be sourced for patients within Ireland, the HSE pays for the patient to be treated abroad (e.g. the UK). Alternately, some people turn to medical tourism in order to receive prompt and cheap treatment.

Tips

- Establishing you are eligible for Irish health services does not automatically mean that your dependants are also eligible.

Public Healthcare

If you are eligible to receive the HSE service, then you are entitled to either full eligibility (Category 1: Medical Card holders) or limited eligibility (Category 2: Non medical card holders).

Category 1: Irish Medical Card Holders

If you are an Irish resident and low income earner, then you may be entitled to a medical card. Medical card holders receive a range of health services free of charge such as:

- GP visits
- Drug and medicine prescriptions (some charges may apply)
- Hospital services
- Dental, optical and aural services
- Maternity and infant care
- Community care and personal social services

If you are eligible for a medical card, then your dependant spouse or partner and children are also usually covered.

Even if you do not qualify for a medical card due to your income, you may still qualify for a GP visit card.

Category 2: Non-Medical Card Holders

You are entitled to receive public hospital services, but you may have to pay inpatient and outpatient hospital charges. You will also receive:

- Subsidised prescription drugs.
- Free maternity care.
- Free or subsidised community care and personal social services.

Unless you hold a GP visit card you will need to pay for your GP visits.

General Practitioners

In Ireland, a general practitioner, or GP, is a doctor who works from a private surgery and/or patients home rather than a hospital.

Patients with a Medical Card

Those that have a medical card need to register with a GP who have registered to see patients under this scheme. If you do not qualify for a medical card due to your income, you may still qualify for a GP visit card.

Patients with a GP Visit Card

A GP visit card allows you to visit participating GP's for free. However, you will still need to pay for prescriptions and hospital charges.

GP Visits for Children Under 6 Years and People over 70 Years

From 2015, all children under six years of age and people over 70 years of age are entitled to free GP visits.

GP Visits for All Others

If you are not eligible for any of the above entitlements, you are considered a private patient and can register with any GP that offers services to private patients. A GP visit can set you back €40 to €70. You should confirm the charges with your GP when you register as they can vary all over the country. If you have health insurance it may cover GP visits or even subsidise them, so check your level of cover with your health insurer.

Tips

- When moving to Ireland, remember to get a copy of your medical history as well as any prescriptions to assist you in continuing your healthcare in Ireland.

Specialist Services

To get access to a specialist, you need to be referred by your GP. They will refer you to the local specialist either in the nearest city or regional hospital. Unless you pay the full private fees or have health insurance then it can take some time sitting on the public health system waitlist before you get to see a specialist.

If you live in a regional area and require specialty care, you may need to travel to a city hospital to receive the specialised treatment you need.

Emergency Services

The Irish Public Healthcare system provides ambulance services to transport the seriously ill to hospitals. Unless you have a medical card, you may be charged for this service, depending on your circumstances.

Ireland's public and private hospitals have Accident and Emergency (A&E) departments for serious emergencies. Be aware that if you attend a private hospital, you will be charged accordingly.

At Irish public hospitals, visiting EU/EEA and Swiss nationals receive emergency care free of charge. However, if you do not come under one of these categories then you will need to pay for the cost of your treatment. If you are an Irish resident then unless you hold a medical card, there may be some costs for your visit. However, the costs are very reasonable, especially when compared with countries like the USA. Alternately, you could consider getting health insurance.

When you arrive at the A&E you will be prioritised on the basis of medical need. Therefore, non-urgent cases may be required to wait for treatment, so you may be better off going to see your GP rather than sitting in an A&E waiting room for hours.

Tips

- Dial 999 or 112 for an ambulance in an emergency.

Long Term Illnesses

Those who are eligible for the Long Term Illness Scheme can receive free drugs and medicines for their condition, regardless of whether or not they hold a medical card.

Children's Healthcare

From 2015, all children under six years of age are entitled to free GP visits.

Children also receive free vaccinations including Tuberculosis, Diphtheria, Tetanus, Whooping cough (Pertussis), HiB (Haemophilus influenzae B), Polio, Meningitis C, Measles, Mumps and Rubella. Girls also receive the HPV vaccination at 12 years of age.

Women's Healthcare

Cervical Check

Ireland provides a free smear test program called Cervical Check. This program is available to residents of Ireland and provides free smear tests to women aged 25 to 60.

For more information go to the Cervical Check website *cervicalcheck.ie*.

Breast Check

Ireland provides a free breast cancer screening program to residents of Ireland aged 50 to 64. The program is called Breast Check and it provides screening a free mammogram on an area-by-area basis every two years.

For more information go to the Breast Check website *breastcheck.ie*.

Abortion

Abortion is a controversial topic in the Republic of Ireland and it is currently illegal unless there is a real and substantial risk to the mother's life.

Women seeking to undergo an abortion typically travel to Britain where it is legal. Northern Ireland is not included in the UK's Abortion Act of 1967. Although not illegal, abortion is generally only permitted where there is a serious threat to the health of the woman.

Maternity Care

All women who are eligible to receive Irish public health services receive free maternity care through the Maternity and Infant Health Care Scheme, regardless of whether they hold a medical card. Only treatment relating to the pregnancy is covered by the scheme.

Women can give birth either in a hospital or at home and have access to pain relief options such as Epidurals. Breast feeding is encouraged and consequently there is support to assist new mothers with this. Ireland also provides new mothers with free public health nurse home visits and support from the Community Mothers Program through local GPs.

It is a legal requirement that you officially register the birth within three months. The Register of Births form is usually given to parents in the hospital and it needs to be completed by one of the parents and signed and submitted at the Office of the Registrar. There is no fee for registering a birth.

If the parents of the child are Irish citizens, then the child automatically qualifies as an Irish citizen. However, a baby born to foreign nationals or British or Northern Irish parents does not automatically qualify for Irish citizenship.

Tips

- Antenatal classes are commonplace and are run at all major Irish maternity hospitals as well as on a private basis.

Contact your local hospital for information on classes. For private services, a quick internet search will lead you to services in your area.

- You can find information and support about home births through the Home Birth Association of Ireland *homebirth.ie*.
- For information about Doula services, see Doula Ireland *doulaireland.com*.

Sexual Health Services

In Ireland, you can get sexual health advice and support services and contraception from the following services:

GP's

Unless you have a medical card or a GP visit card, then visiting your GP for contraception can be expensive. A GP visit can set you back €40 to €70. Consequently, many of the long acting contraceptive options such as the IUD and implants are becoming more popular in Ireland.

Family Planning Clinics

These clinics are often cheaper than seeing a private practice GP and also typically have student and unemployed rates.

Online

For a fee, you can get your contraceptive pill prescription online, and even order a STI Test Kit to be sent to your home. However, online doctors do not give you the opportunity for face to face discussion about your personal medical circumstances.

- Lloyds Online Doctor *lloydsonlinedoctor.ie*
- Webdoctor *Webdoctor.ie*
- Superdrug *onlinedoctor.superdrug.com/ie*
- Dr Ed *dred.com/ie*

Contraceptive Options in Ireland

All contraceptive devices are available in Ireland, including:
- Contraceptive pill and mini pill

- Injectable contraception
- Coil
- Intrauterine System (IUS)
- Implant
- Patch
- Vaginal ring
- Diaphragms / cap
- Female and male condoms

Condoms are readily available from supermarkets, convenience stores and pharmacies. Condoms can be quite pricey in Ireland. Many college student services give them out for free or cheap.

How to Obtain the Emergency Contraceptive Pill in Ireland

Also called the morning after pill, there are several types of emergency contraceptive pills available in Ireland.

- *NorLevo:* Available over the counter from pharmacists (no need to see a GP or get a prescription) and can be taken up to three days (72 hours) after unprotected sex.
- *EllaOne:* Is only available on prescription from a GP or Family Planning Clinic. It can be taken up to 5 days (120 hours) after unprotected sex.

How to Obtain the Contraceptive Pill in Ireland

Pharmacists cannot dispense the contraceptive pill without a prescription from a registered Irish GP. GP's can only prescribe six months worth of contraceptive pill at a time.

The brand name on the label of your pill may not be familiar to Irish GP's, so it helps if you bring along the packaging that states the actual chemical ingredients and prescribed dosage. Be aware that the type of pill that you take may not be available in Ireland, but your GP should be able to work with you to find an alternative that suits your needs.

A cheap way to get a contraceptive pill prescription without having to pay to see a GP is to obtain it from an online Irish pharmacy for around €20 – €25. However, this does not give you the opportunity for a face to face discussion with a GP, so may not suit everyone.

On the website you will be given a range of contraceptive pills to choose from and then asked to complete an online consultation. Then, after paying the fee, you will be sent a prescription for your contraceptive pill from a registered Irish GP. You then take this prescription to any pharmacy to have it filled.

Online pharmacies that provide contraceptive pill prescriptions:
- Lloyds Online Doctor *lloydsonlinedoctor.ie*
- Webdoctor *Webdoctor.ie*
- Superdrug *onlinedoctor.superdrug.com/ie*
- Dr Ed *dred.com/ie*

Medicines and Pharmacies

Pharmacies are widely available in Irish towns and cities. Opening hours are usually 9am to 6pm or 8pm, Monday to Saturday. Some are open till late (10pm) during the week and on Sundays. There are no 24/7 pharmacies and if medication is required urgently, it's best to go to the emergency department of you nearest hospital.

Pharmacists cannot dispense drugs without a prescription from a registered Irish doctor. Before moving to Ireland, get a list of your medications from your doctor. Remember, the brand name on the label of your medications may not be familiar to Irish GP's and pharmacists, so it helps to bring along the packaging that states the actual chemical ingredients and your prescribed dosage.

Everyday drugs such as paracetamol and ibuprofen are very expensive to purchase in Ireland. Furthermore, due to the high numbers of recorded paracetamol overdose in Ireland it is against the law for shops to sell paracetamol in blister packs of more than 12 (500 mg) tablets in a single transaction, and in pharmacies they cannot sell more than a 24 pack. For doses higher than this, they can only sell half this amount. Drugs containing codeine can only be sold in pharmacies over the counter.

Because of the high cost of medications, many people purchase them online. However, be aware that it is illegal to import prescription drugs and drugs (including supplements) that are banned in Ireland. Consequently they can be seized by customs.

Saving Money on Your Prescriptions in Ireland

There is no Value Added Taxes charged on oral medications in Ireland.

Shop Around

Both the retail price of the medication as well as the pharmacy's fee to dispense the medicines can vary greatly between pharmacies. You can save money by shopping around to get the best price. To save time and energy, simply phone the pharmacy to check the total price that they charge to fill your prescription.

Buy in Bulk

Buying in bulk is another great way to save money. If there is an option to dispense your prescription in bulk (for example, collecting a 6 month supply instead of collecting it twice as 3 months supply), then this is usually cheaper as you will only have to pay the dispensing fee once.

Drugs Payment Scheme

Without a medical card you will need to pay for your medications as well as the pharmacists dispensing fee. However, if you are under the Drugs Payment Scheme, the limit for an individual or family is €144 per month. Anyone who is an Irish resident and holds a PPSN can apply for this scheme.

To register for the Drugs Payment Scheme, go to your Local Health Office.

Vitamin and Supplements

Ireland has tight restrictions on the sale of vitamins and supplements (including herbal). Many are either banned outright or banned from being sold over the counter and may only be obtained via a prescription.

Medical Tourism

Each year thousands of Irish make their way abroad to seek discount medical procedures from essential surgeries to cosmetic surgery and dentistry. Hungary, Spain, Poland, Czech Republic,

Belgium, Turkey, Spain and Thailand are just some of the many countries that Irish turn to, especially those tired of waiting on long waitlists for medical procedures in Ireland. The idea of combining a holiday with medical treatment can be particularly attractive, but you need to be careful and thoroughly do your research before deciding on where to go.

Private Health Insurance

Although Ireland's public health system offers treatment at a significantly reduced rate, the long waitlists turn many Irish to private health insurance. Tax relief is available for premiums paid for health insurance. Some employers may provide health insurance as part of their employment package.

All private health insurance providers are registered with the Health Insurance Authority which is the country's independent regulator for private health insurance. They also provide information about your rights, and advice about how to select your plan.

Providers:
- VHI (Voluntary Health Insurance) *vhi.ie*
- Laya Healthcare *layahealthcare.ie*
- Aviva Health *avivahealth.ie*
- GloHealth *glohealth.ie*

Irish Private Health Insurance Regulations

Health insurance providers that offer inpatient hospital services must provide a minimum level of benefits:
- Day care / in-patient treatment.
- Hospital out-patient treatment.
- Maternity benefits.
- Convalescence.
- Psychiatric treatment and substance abuse.
- The minimum accommodation level is semi-private in a public hospital.

Although your treatment may be privately funded, you may find yourself receiving treatment at a public hospital. That's because the public hospitals provide a number of private or semi-private beds to boost their income. Consequently, you will be treated as a private patient and charged the full cost for the services provided.

Health insurance companies must provide you lifetime cover. This means that they cannot refuse to provide you cover. They must also accept anyone who wishes to join regardless of their age, sex or health status, but you will be subject to waiting periods before the cover takes effect. However, if you have already served this time with another insurer you do not need to do so again when transferring to another provider.

Unlike other insurances such as motor or life insurance, your age, sex, health or past record of claims does not affect the price that you will be charged for your health insurance. Therefore, all adults pay equally for the same amount of benefits. However, charges for people aged under 18, people aged 18 to 23 who are in full-time education, retired people who have a special arrangement within their company's health insurance scheme and people in group health insurance schemes may all be on a lower rate than the normal adult rate.

Irish Private Health Insurance Lifetime Community Rating

From 1 May 2015, higher charges apply to people who are 35 years of age or older when they first take out health insurance. There will be a 2% loading for each year over 34 years of age. If you are not insured on 1 May 2015 but previously had health insurance, you can be given credit for the time you were insured, reducing the number of years to which the loading applies. If you stopped your insurance cover for periods of unemployment since 1 January 2008, up to three years of credits can be provided.

If you live outside Ireland on 1 May 2015 but subsequently move to live in Ireland, a loading will not apply if you get health insurance within nine months and continue to be insured.

For further details about the lifetime community rating, refer to The Department of Health's list of frequently asked questions on their website *health.gov.ie*.

5 FINANCE

Banking

Before the economic crash, banks offered competitive interest rates and attractive incentives to bank with them. However, the situation is now rather dismal for the consumer. Many banks have since closed, merged or withdrawn their personal banking services. The banks that remain charge high fees and offer little to no interest on their daily accounts. As a newcomer it can even be very difficult to open a bank account.

Choosing a Bank

To avoid paying high fees, look for banks that offer free services if you meet conditions such as, having a minimum amount in your account and/or depositing a minimum monthly amount into your account (this one is usually achievable if you are getting your salary paid into the account).

Banks will usually provide you with a combined ATM and debit card. They also provide internet / online, telephone and mobile phone banking services, however the quality of this service can vary between banks.

ATM's are prevalent in Ireland, but it pays to check whether your new potential bank has plenty of accessible ones in the area that you live in.

Irish Banks

- Bank of Ireland *bankofireland.com*
- Allied Irish Banks (AIB) *aib.ie*
- Ulster Bank *digital.ulsterbank.ie*
- Permanent tsb Group (PTSB) *permanenttsb.ie*
- KBC *kbc.ie*
- Educational Building Society (EBS) *ebs.ie*
- Rabodirect *rabodirect.ie* – An exclusively online bank.

Irish Bank Opening Hours

Banks are open weekdays 9.30am or 10am and close at 4pm or 4.30pm. Most banks have one evening per week where they open until 5pm e.g. in Dublin this is usually on Thursdays.

Most banks open their main branches in town and city areas on Saturdays for reduced hours 10am to 1pm.

Tips

- The Money Guide *moneyguideireland.com* website regularly publish articles comparing Irish banks and their fees.
- Irish often refer to a debit card as a laser card.
- You may want to reconsider your need for a credit card when you find out the annual Government duty charges as outlined below. However, if you are planning on renting a car, a credit card is usually required (but it doesn't have to be an Irish one).
- If you need cash and your bank only allows you a limited number of free withdrawals each month, then withdraw cash from the retailer when purchasing items. Not all retailers offer this, but supermarkets usually do, so use this function when you buy your groceries. When you are about to pay for your goods, ask for the cash amount that you want (be aware that they usually have a maximum cash out of about €100). They will add the cash amount to your total purchase and then hand you the cash with your receipt.

Opening a Bank Account

It can be very difficult to open an Irish bank account when you move to Ireland. It's almost as if nobody wants your money or custom, so make sure that you have other means of accessing your money while waiting for an account to be opened. It can also take up to a week to receive your bank debit card.

One of the main difficulties you will face is being able to produce suitable evidence of your Irish residential address in order to meet the banks rather strict requirements.

What You Will Need to Open a Bank Account in Ireland

1. *Personal details:* An address and Irish mobile phone number.
2. *Photo identification:* Such as a passport or a full Irish drivers licence – they may also accept a full UK drivers licence.
3. *Evidence of your Irish residential address:* Two forms of non-photographic identification. They need to be documents that have your name and residential address on them and they need to be dated within the last 6 months. Accepted forms are:
   - Bank statement or credit card statement (if you are new to Ireland, then this will only work if your bank from your home country has been sending these to you in Ireland).
   - Utility bill e.g. electricity, internet, water.
   - Current household / contents insurance, health insurance or motor insurance certificate.
   - They may also accept your rental agreement as one form of evidence.
4. *PPS Number:* This is not essential when opening an account but they may ask you for it if you are working and paying your salary into the account.

Tips

- Struggling to get evidence of your address? You could get your employer to post an employment confirmation letter to your current Irish address on their company letterhead.
- If you are planning to get health insurance, then sign up as soon as arrive (you could even do this before you arrive if

you already have an Irish address that can receive your mail). They will send you a new membership letter which can then be used as evidence of your address.

Irish Government Stamp Duty Charges

The Government charges a stamp duty on your financial cards i.e. your ATM and debit card. For cards that act as both an ATM and debit card (which most people have), you will be charged a higher duty. Credit card holders get charged an even higher duty.

These duties get automatically charged to your account annually, so there is no avoiding them. Learn more at *revenue.ie*.

Transferring Funds in and out of Ireland

Money Transfers Within the Republic of Ireland

When you open your bank account you will be given a National Sort Code (NSC, but typically referred to as the 'sort code'). This 6 digit code identifies both the bank and the branch where the account is held. If you are transferring money within the Republic of Ireland (e.g. paying your rent), you will be asked to provide your sort code alongside your bank account number. This number is also usually printed on your bank statements.

Money Transfers Outside of the Republic of Ireland, but Within the Single European Payments Area (SEPA)

SEPA countries include all countries that are members of the EU: Austria, Belgium, Bulgaria, Cyprus, Czech Republic, Denmark, Estonia, Finland, France, Germany, Greece, Hungary, Ireland, Italy, Latvia, Lithuania, Luxembourg, Malta, Netherlands, Poland, Portugal, Romania, Slovakia, Slovenia, Spain, Sweden, United Kingdom. It also includes Norway, Iceland, Liechtenstein, Monaco and Switzerland.

If you want to carry out money transfers then you need an account with SEPA capabilities. This is a European Union initiative to simplify the process for bank transfers using the euro.

You will also need to use the banks Business Identifier Code (BIC). This is the address assigned to a bank in order to accurately send automated payments to the bank concerned. It uniquely identifies the name and country (and sometimes the branch) of the bank involved. BICs are often called SWIFT (Society for Worldwide Interbank Financial Telecommunication) Codes and can be either 8 or 11 characters long. SWIFT provides a network that enables financial institutions worldwide to send and receive information about financial transactions in a secure, standardized and reliable environment.

The other number that you will need is an IBAN (International Bank Account Number), which is used internationally to uniquely identify the sort code and account number of a customer at a financial institution.

Your BIC and IBAN numbers should be given to you by the bank when you open your account. You can also find this information on your bank statement.

The Banking and Payments Federation Ireland website *bpfi.ie* also provides a BIC & IBAN conversion tool which will convert any domestic sort code and account number to its equivalent BIC & IBAN.

International Money Transfers outside of the Single European Payments Area (SEPA)

The easiest, safest, and cheapest way to carry out international money transfers to or from countries outside of the SEPA is via:
- International money exchange companies
- At a bank
- At any An Post office branch

Typically, the more that you transfer, the better the rate you will get. Be sure to shop around to get the best rate and look out for companies that may have hidden fees. If you are transferring large amounts of money, then many international money exchange companies waive the fees which can save you a lot of money.

Income Taxes

The Irish Income Tax System

Employees pay income tax through the Irish PAYE (Pay As You Earn) system. The PAYE system means that your employer deducts the tax that you owe directly from your wages prior to paying you. Your employer gives this tax directly to the Revenue Commissioners.

Tips

- The financial / fiscal / budget year in Ireland matches the calendar year, 1 January to 31 December.

Am I Liable to Pay Tax in Ireland?

If you have spent 183 or more days in the tax year or 280 days over two years living in Ireland, then you are considered a resident for tax purposes. If you are out of Ireland for 30 days or less, it won't be counted towards the 280 days. This means that you will be expected to pay tax on your income inside and outside of Ireland. On the other hand, non-residents only have to pay taxes on their income inside Ireland.

Be aware that Irish residents are liable to pay tax on both their Irish income as well as their foreign income, including foreign pensions. They are also liable for taxation in the foreign country, however, Ireland has double taxation agreements with a number of countries. Refer to the Tax Treaties section of the Irish Revenue website *revenue.ie*. You can obtain tax relief if your country of residence is among them.

How Do I Pay Tax in Ireland?

As soon as you get a job, you need to apply to the Department of Social Protection for a Personal Public Service Number (PPSN). Once you receive your PPSN, give it to your employer.

You then need to apply for a certificate of tax credits by completing the tax Form 12A which you can get from your employer or from the Irish Revenue Department website *revenue.ie*. Take the time to complete this Form 12A honestly and accurately and renew it if your circumstances change, otherwise you could find yourself in trouble for falsely claiming tax credits as the Revenue department carries out regular revenue audits.

Once completed, the Form 12A needs to be given to the local tax office. They will then send you a certificate of tax credits and provide a copy to your employer so that they can correctly tax your pay. If you don't get this completed, then eventually your employer will have to apply the much higher emergency tax rate until you have this in place.

What Are Irish Tax Credits?

Tax credits reduce the amount of income tax that you are required to pay. The tax credits you receive are dependent on your personal circumstances, for example, the single person tax credit and married person's tax credits. For more information, visit the Irish Revenue Department website *revenue.ie*.

What Are the Tax Rates in Ireland?

The amount of tax that you pay depends on your personal circumstances and the tax credits that you are eligible for. For the current tax rates, visit the Irish Revenue Department website *revenue.ie*.

Irish Tax Returns

Your employer will give you a P60 at the end of the year. The P60 is a statement of your wages and the total tax that you have paid for the year. If you have not earned any other income during the financial year, you may not have to file a tax return. However, you can opt to complete the tax Form 12 in order to claim tax relief on tax credits and allowances like medical expenses. You can obtain this form from the tax office or the Irish Revenue Department website *revenue.ie*.

However, you must to lodge a self-assessed tax return if you are a:
- Contractor
- Subcontractor
- Self-employed
- Company director
- Landlord
- Receive other income in addition to your PAYE income e.g. investments.
- Belong to an employee share scheme.

You can lodge your tax return by sending it into the tax office. Alternately, you can lodge your tax return online using the Revenues On-Line Service (ROS). In order to use this service you must complete the ROS registration process. You will then be issued a personal ROS access number in the mail which will enable you to file your tax return online. After lodging your tax return, the tax office will provide you with a statement of your tax liability called a P21.

Important

- You must submit your tax return by 31 August.
- You must pay any outstanding taxes for the previous tax year by 31 October.
- There are penalties that apply for lodging a late tax return.

Tips

- Utilising an online Tax Return company is often cheaper than visiting one.
- If you have been unemployed for four weeks or more, you may be eligible for a tax refund. To apply, complete a Form P50 which is available from the tax office or the Irish Revenue Department website *revenue.ie*.

What Is a P21?

A P21 is your statement from the tax office that displays:
- Your total income for the financial year.
- Your tax credits.
- The total tax that you have paid for the financial year.

The statement will advise you on whether you have overpaid or underpaid your taxes for the financial year. If you are applying for a loan or mortgage, you may need to give your P21 to the bank as proof of your earnings.

What Happens if I Have Overpaid or Underpaid Tax?

If you have overpaid tax, it will be paid to you either by cheque or into your bank account if you have given Revenue your bank details. If you have not paid enough tax, then you can pay the

outstanding amount by:
- Posting your payment in the pre-paid envelope that will have been provided with your P21.
- Pay it in person at the Collectors-Generals office.
- Pay by bank transfer.

Important

- You must pay any outstanding tax by 31 October otherwise you will be charged interest on the amount owing.

What Happens When I Leave My Employment?

Your employer must give you a P45, which is a statement of your pay and how much tax that they have deducted. This form is essential and must be given to your new employer. If you have become unemployed, you will need the P45 to claim a tax refund and to apply for social welfare benefits.

What Do I Do If I'm Leaving the Country?

Make sure that you obtain your P45 from your employer. You may be eligible for a tax refund. To apply, complete the tax Form P50 which is available from your local tax office and the Irish Revenue Department website *revenue.ie*.

6 HOUSING

What to Expect from Irish Housing

When moving to Ireland, be prepared for the housing to be different from what you may previously be used to. This guide provides you an overview of what to expect as well as a detailed explanation on how to use the Irish energy and heating systems.

Flats versus Apartments

If you are looking for cheap accommodation, then a flat may be the best option. Flats are converted from older houses and are typically self contained, but some may share facilities such as the laundry, or even living areas. Often the layout can be awkward and cramped and the kitchen usually consists of a tiny bench. In some flats you may pay a fixed amount for the utilities (e.g. electricity, waste) each month, but in others you may have to arrange and pay for them yourself. Parking is not usually included, but there may be street parking options.

Purpose built apartments are usually a bit more expensive, but roomier with a better lay out. Billing for utilities would typically be separate for each apartment, but they may have a shared waste service.

Houses

City houses are typically three to four bedroom and semi-detached (two houses attached by a central wall). In the city areas, houses are usually terraced or rowhouse (house joined to another on either side of it). Free standing or detached houses are more common in towns and villages.

Security

Consider the security of the property. If you are living in a city area, then you need to understand that there is a reasonably high risk of being broken into. Ground floor or basement apartments are often cheaper, but they usually experience more break-ins and as a result you are usually charged more for insurance.

Insurance

The landlord must insure the property. However, this only covers the damage to the structure, i.e. the bricks and mortar. It is the tenant's responsibility to get contents insurance to protect their personal belongings.

Furnishings

It is common for rental properties to come furnished. The quality and amount of furnishing varies, but typically properties come with the basics (couch, bed, table and chairs, whiteware, basic kitchenware), but don't usually include electronics such as a TV. You will need to supply your own bedding and towels.

Kitchen

Unless you find a modern property or have a big rental budget, most kitchens can be quite small in Ireland.

Most city rentals only come with a mini bar / under the counter style fridge (especially in flats). If this does not suit your needs then remember to check if the property has a full size fridge freezer before viewing so you don't waste your time.

Dishwashers: Most modern and renovated properties tend to come with one. However, many older builds have tiny kitchens that won't accommodate one.

Storage: Pantry storage is not very common in Ireland. So when considering your rental, make sure that it has enough kitchen storage for both your kitchenware and food stores.

Laundry

It's quite common for these to be located in the kitchen and for the machine to be a combination washer and dryer. However, don't assume and be sure to check this out.

Storage

Does it have a built in wardrobe or does it come furnished with a wardrobe and set of drawers? If not, this may be something that you have to purchase.

Is there enough room to store your belongings such as suitcases and other junk? Most places offer general storage in the cupboard where the hot water tank is stored, however, this space can vary from tiny to spacious. These are usually located by the front door, which makes them a great place to store jackets and shoes.

Property Orientation

South facing is the best for all day sun, but these can be hard to find and more expensive.

West facing is a good alternate option. It will give your property afternoon sun which can be very warming. However, if the property doesn't have many windows then this could be void.

Consider downloading a compass app for your phone to help you determine the properties direction.

Parking

Be aware that some properties won't come with parking, especially in city areas. Off street parking may be available in modern apartments, however, not all of them include parking as part of your rent. You may be charged an additional monthly fee to secure a car park. Other properties may be in areas where you need to purchase a local council parking permit.

Waste

If you are living in an apartment complex, waste removal is usually included in your rent. They would typically provide large waste skips for you to use. In flats, sometimes the landlord provides a shared bin. However, if you are living in a house, it would usually be your responsibility to pay for rubbish collection as it is a pay for service in Ireland.

Always ask the leasing agent about the rubbish collection arrangements, as you may need to add this cost to your budget.

Energy

In Ireland, there are no electrical outlets in the bathrooms. Sockets are not allowed in bathrooms or shower rooms unless they are fitted at least three metres from the bath or shower, but occasionally you may find a shaver-supply unit installed.

Some properties may have access to gas, but electricity is typically the main source of energy.

Some flats charge for utilities in a set monthly fee either added to or included in the rent. Other flats may be set up so that the individual tenant is responsible for the utilities. Some flats may even use a prepay electricity service.

Heating

It gets cold in the winter, so make sure you look for a property with good insulation and double glazing to help keep you warm and cut down on heating bills. Older properties can be very cold if they have not been renovated with improved insulation. Some double glazed windows in modern buildings may also come with air vents. These are great for allowing circulation of air in cooler months. Properties would not normally come with air conditioning because it does not get hot enough in the summer to warrant any. Usually a fan will suffice.

Some properties, especially older ones, may have working fireplaces. In Ireland, a popular and cheap form of fuel is bog peat. The peat is compressed into bricks and you can buy them from the supermarkets and local stores. It can be very hard to get a fire started using these peat bricks, so try cutting them into slivers and use dry wood and kindling and fire starters to help get it lit.

Some modern homes may have solar panels installed and also underfloor heating. Underfloor heating is absolute bliss, especially in the bathroom.

In Ireland, there are a number of different ways to heat your home and water. This can be very confusing if you have not had experience with these systems before. Below is an outline of the main types of heating. If you are unsure how to use your system, get your landlord to explain it to you.

Night Storage Heaters

A common form of efficient heating is night storage heaters (aka night store or heat bank). They turn on during the night to take advantage of the cheaper night time electricity rates. The night store heaters work by storing thermal energy, which is released during the day via thermal radiation to keep your house toasty warm. These heaters usually have an output and input function for you to control how much heat is stored and how fast you want it released during the day. However, in newer models, they may not have these controls as this function may be automatic.

If it's not cold enough to use the night store function, these heaters usually have the option to also use them as a normal heater for instant heat.

In winter-time, the "off peak" electricity in winter is from 11pm to 8am. In summer-time the night-rate hours are midnight until 9am. You should not need to make changes to the timer, as they usually are set up automatically for both summer and winter times.

To get the night store heaters to work, they will have two electrical switches. One will be for using the heater during the day as a normal heater, the other will be for using the night store function. If the switches have indicator lights, then the switch for the night store heater will not turn on until the night time rate kicks in. Be aware that many modern apartments in Ireland do not use night store heaters in the bedrooms. These are usually just normal heaters, sometimes with timer functions.

Boilers

Boilers are used to heat both the home and the water. You can run a gas, oil, LPG or wood chip or pellet boiler, depending on what fuel source is accessible to you.

Combi Boiler

This boiler provides limitless, on demand hot water as well as heat to your radiators (the heaters in your home) directly from your main water supply. These can be economical since they only heat the water you use. The boiler itself is quite small since there is no need to have a separate hot or cold water tank, and are typically used in smaller homes.

Conventional and System Boilers

This type of boiler sends heated water to your radiators and hot water cylinder. These boilers suit larger family homes. So that you don't have to wait for the water to heat, you can use the programmable timer function to have it ready when you need it most. You may also have an immersion system installed as a backup in case the boiler breaks down.

Water Heating Systems

Immersion Heaters

Immersion heaters are a common form of water heating in Irish households. An immersion heater is an electric heater that sits inside the hot water cylinder. It has a heating coil inside of it, and, similar to a kettle, you turn it on to heat up the water prior to using it. Then, once you've finished with it, you need to remember to turn it off otherwise it just keeps heating the water which uses a lot of electricity.

More modern immersion systems have additional features such as:

- Set time function – enable you to turn it on for a set time e.g. 30 minute, one hour, two hours, after which it turns itself off.
- Programmable timer – allows you to set it to turn on at a set time, for a set amount of time. Time-of-use tariff users can use this function to set their timer to turn on during off-peak cheaper hours.
- Thermostatic control which switches off the immersion once it reaches a certain temperature.
- Well insulated to keep the water hot for many hours.

Unfortunately many older properties have just the basic immersion system. That means not only do you need to remember to turn it on before your shower or bath (plan ahead, because it will need time to heat up), but then after you're done, you need to remember to turn it off or face a large electricity bill. This is one of the most common forms of household arguments – "Who the feck left the immersion on?!".

Tips

- The Irish call the cupboard that stores the immersion heater, the 'hot press'. 'Press' is a term they use to describe cupboards, and 'hot' – because the hot water is in there.
- You need to ensure that your immersion heater is reaching temperatures above 50°C to kill bacteria.

Night Storage Water Heater

These systems turn on during the night to take advantage of the cheaper night time electricity rates. The "off peak" electricity in winter is from 11pm to 8am. In summer time the night-rate hours are midnight until 9am. Depending on your system, you should not need to make changes to the timer, as they are set up automatically. However, these dials are usually openly accessible, so you may want to check that no one has unwittingly changed it. Having it set to the wrong time could cause it to turn on during the high-peak, expensive time of the day, costing you money.

There is usually one dial with two markers, one labelled 'Summer Time' and the other labelled 'Winter Time'. The time on the dial should be set at the actual time of day for the season that you are in. The water tank itself must also be surrounded by a thick layer of insulation to keep the water warm as long as possible.

These type of water heaters usually also have a 'Boost' setting, which is an immersion system alongside it. This enables you to have access to hot water when the water in the main tank has begun cooling down in the evening. This boost setting is typically a timer function. They are usually quite efficient, and, although my boost timer can run for two hours, I find I only need to set it to heat for about 20 minutes in order to get a hot shower.

The downsides to this kind of system is if your family typically uses the bulk of their hot water in the evening, as they are really set up to be most useful in the morning. Consequently, you may end up having to use the boost system in the evening which will increase your energy costs.

Tips

- To save money, turn your water heating off while you are away on holiday. But don't forget to set a reminder in your phone to turn it back on when you arrive home! However, don't panic if you forget, you can still use the boost option if you need hot water before it has had a chance to heat up overnight.

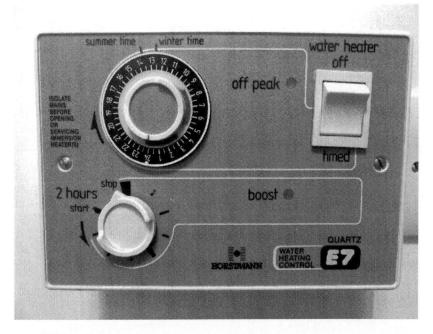

Night storage water heater with immersion 'boost' option

Electric Showers

Some homes may have an electric shower installed. Basically it looks like a large white box attached to the shower wall with dials. These are great if you rely on immersion heating because you don't have to worry about preheating the water in order to have a hot shower.

Inside the electric shower box is a small tank that has a powerful heating element, much like a kettle, which instantly heats the water. To operate the electric shower, you will need to turn on the mains switch first - usually via a pull cord which will be beside a pilot light that will tell you whether it is on or off. Then on the electric shower box there will be an 'on' switch which will start the water coming out of the shower head. Turn the temperature dial to adjust the water heat which uses a scale running from blue (cold) to red (hot). In wintertime when the water temperature drops, the electric shower needs to work much harder so you will find yourself having to turn the heat up and may also notice a drop in water pressure. On some models there is also a dial to adjust the water pressure.

For an electric shower to work effectively, you need a cold water supply with reasonably high water pressure because the shower heating unit will reduce the pressure of the water as it flows through. So some showers may also have a power shower fitted. It takes in and heats cold water just like an ordinary electric shower, but it also uses an electric pump to increase the water pressure so it leaves the nozzle with greater force and higher speed. However, the down side to these particular units is that they can be very noisy.

Property Checklist

Preparation and forethought is the key to finding the right accommodation for you. Below is a checklist template that can be used to help guide you in your property search.

- Apartment or house?
- If you have pets, does the landlord allow them? (Make sure this is included in the rental agreement.)
- Furnished or unfurnished?
- Full sized fridge freezer or mini bar style fridge?
- Dishwasher?
- Washing machine and dryer?
- Adequate storage?
- Linen closet?
- Number of bedrooms?

- Bathroom – bath or shower? Or both?
- What is the properties orientation? How much sun will it get?
- Reasonable heating options?
- Double glazing? Double glazing can reduce your heating bills in the cooler months and reduce outside noise.
- Is it on a busy road? Double glazing can help reduce the traffic noise.
- Internet connections?
- Waste options? Check whose responsibility it is to pay waste charges.
- Are all appliances and facilities working properly?
- Are there any signs of dampness in the property?
- Do you want a communal garden / private garden / balcony?
- Is there a good supermarket nearby?
- Amenities: Do you want to be close to bars, restaurants, movie theatre etc..?
- Close to transport options and accessible to the airport?
- Parking options?
- How much is the deposit and what are the conditions of its return to you?

Tips

- Find out more hints and tips for problem free renting from Ireland's Private Residential Tenancies Board website, *prtb.ie*.

Renting Accommodation

Finding a suitable place to live once you arrive in Ireland is one of the most important first steps to getting settled. Initially, you should consider staying in short term accommodation for a month or two to give yourself time to settle in to your new job and to familiarise yourself with the local area. Then, once you find the area that you would prefer to live in, start searching for a suitable property.

Step 1: How Much Rent Can You Afford?

Deposit: You will need to pay a deposit up front – usually the equivalent of one month's rent.

Rent: The rent is usually paid on a monthly basis and you will also be required to pay your first months rent up front. So make sure you have enough cash available!

Utilities: It is typically the tenant's responsibility to pay for utilities, so ensure that you include this when working out your budget and deciding how much you can afford for rent. Those living in flats may pay a fixed amount for some of the utilities each month, but in others you may have to arrange and pay for them yourself.

Typical utilities you can expect to pay in Ireland:

- Electricity or gas or both
- Water
- Waste
- Annual TV licence (an Irish Government requirement if you have a TV)
- Parking (if you plan to purchase a car)
- Contents insurance
- Internet and phone
- Mobile phone
- Subscription pay TV (optional)

Step 2: What Do You Want from Your Rented Accommodation?

You should make a list of the 'must haves' that you want from your property like e.g. a bath, a dishwasher etc…. We all have different needs. Refer to my 'Property Checklist' to get you started. I've also put together a list of what you can expect from a rental property in Ireland, refer to 'What to Expect from Irish Housing'.

Step 3: Where Is Your Preferred Area?

The only way to find your favourite (and affordable) area/s is to go and visit them and have a good walk or cycle around. What sort of bars and restaurants are available? Are there parks, gyms and supermarkets nearby? Make your own list of the type of places that you would like to live close to.

Once you have found your area/s of preference, make sure that you also visit it in the evening to see how safe they feel. Talk to the locals and find out what the area is like to live in.

Step 4: Prepare Your Paperwork

In order to apply for a rental property, there are a number of documents that you will need to provide. Prepare your paperwork in advance and have it with you when you view properties so that you can immediately lodge your application as soon an you find your favourite property.

You will need copies of the following:
- Your ID (your passport if you don't have any Irish ID).
- Previous rental references.
- Work reference from your current employee.
- Evidence of your current employment and income.

Tips
- If you are looking for accommodation in a high demand area, then carry these documents around with you to every viewing so that you can immediately lodge your application and beat the competition!

Step 5: Property Searching

Properties are usually rented out by a property manager or the owner. To view a property, follow the instructions as directed on the advert. Some agents give you an individual viewing time, so make sure that you are there on time.

Once you have viewed a few properties, you will start to get a feel for the type of properties available and what you can expect for your budget.

The best way to begin your search for a rental property is to use the following websites:

Short Term Rental Accommodation in Ireland
- Daft *daft.ie*

- Rent *rent.ie*
- Gumtree *gumtree.ie*
- Air BnB *airbnb.ie*
- My Home *myhome.ie*

Long Term Rental Accommodation in Ireland

- Daft *daft.ie*
- Rent *rent.ie*
- Property *property.ie*
- My Home *myhome.ie*
- Gumtree *gumtree.ie*

Shared Rental Accommodation in Ireland

If you have a small budget, then have you considered sharing a room? There are a number of sites that will help you find shared accommodation:

- Gumtree *gumtree.ie*
- Roomster *roomster.com*

Tips

- If you have pets, be aware that not all landlords will permit them.
- Leasing agents are typically punctual, so make a good impression by attending the property viewing as per the agreed time.
- When viewing properties, discuss with the Property Manager what you are looking for as they may have other suitable properties available. Ask them to contact you when they have other suitable properties come onto the market.
- In University areas, rental properties can be harder to find in August and September because this is the start of the University year and lots of students will be looking for accommodation.

Step 6: What to Do When You've Found a Place You Like

If you are looking in an area with limited vacancies then once you have found a property that you like, you need to be quick.

While you are at the viewing, you need to clearly state your intentions of wanting to rent the property. Give them your prepared documents (see above) and make arrangements to pay the deposit (make sure you get a receipt for this). Typically you would pay your deposit in cash.

Unfortunately in areas of high demand, if the property is reasonably nice it often gets snapped up during the first viewing so you will need to be decisive. Rental selection typically works on a 'first in first served' basis. This means that the first suitable person to lodge their application for the property will be the one that gets it.

If you have pets that will be living with you, make sure that the landlord has agreed to it and have it specified in the lease before signing it.

Tips

- You are not expected to enter into a 'bidding war' and offer more than the advertised rent.

How Long Should I Sign the Rental Lease For?

You also need to decide how long you want to lease the property for. Most landlords require you to be contracted for a minimum stay. This can be anywhere from one month to one year. If you do not know how long you are staying, consider negotiating a short minimum stay so that you are not tied into a contract for too long in case your circumstances change. Sometimes relocations don't go to plan and its best that you consider this before signing up for a long lease, otherwise, breaking your lease could end in you losing your deposit.

If you are planning on buying your own home, consider renting for at least six months to give you time to establish your preferred areas and also a chance to suss out the property market.

Rental Disputes

Ireland has a Private Residential Tenancies Board (PRTB) which resolves disputes between landlords and tenants and also operates the National Tenancy Registration System. All landlords must register their tenancies with the PRTB. Once registered, you will receive a letter in the mail with a unique identifying number. You need to keep this number safe as you will need it if you ever need to deal with the PRTB. Their website, *prtb.ie*, also contains lots of useful information as well as details about your rights, responsibilities, and obligations as a tenant.

Tips

- In Ireland, rentals are commonly referred to as 'lettings', so property agents are usually called 'Letting Agents'.

Rental Scams

There are a lot of online rental property scams and they often target those moving from overseas. After supposed satisfactory e-mails, tenants are asked to send money to the 'landlord'. But when the tenants attempt to make contact with the 'landlord' or collect keys to the property, the 'landlord' is not contactable and the potential tenant has been defrauded. This scamming doesn't just happen online, there are also scammers that will show you an apartment, take your cash up front and then never be seen or heard from again.

If booking short term accommodation online, carefully check the reviews posted from previous guests. Also, be wary of communication in broken English and anyone asking for money upfront. You should also check that the person actually works for a legitimate rental agency, and is not just pretending to be from one.

Buying a Home

The process of buying a home in Ireland can be lengthy and there are many costs involved, for example, mortgage costs, legal fees, registration of deeds and stamp duty. You should only consider buying a property in Ireland once you can afford it and if you plan on staying for a reasonable length of time. Otherwise it may not be a sound financial move and you could risk losing money.

Decide How Much You Can Afford to Spend

Make sure that you include not only the cost of the house, but also the other additional costs such as solicitor fees and stamp duty.

Meet with banks and mortgage brokers to get a mortgage approval in principal to help you establish how much you can afford to spend.

There are many different types of mortgages, so contact a number of different mortgage providers to find out who can offer you the best deal. Otherwise, consider using a mortgage broker.

House Hunting

In Ireland, you need to do the bulk of the house hunting yourself. Real Estate Agents will show you properties that they have listed, but not what other agents have listed.

Once you've decided on your ideal location, the best place to start searching is in local papers and online. Try property websites such as *Daft.ie*, *Rent.ie*, *Property.ie*, *Myhome.ie*, and *Gumtree.ie*. Create search alerts so that properties in your search criteria are emailed to you as soon as they are listed. You should also make contact with the local Real Estate Agents operating in your preferred areas and register with them. Hopefully they will contact you when they have something suitable for viewing, but you can't rely on this, so continue your own search.

When carrying out house viewings, have a property checklist with you to help guide you in your decision making process. In addition, look at the homes Building Energy Rating (BER). The BER will provide you information about how energy-efficient the home is. You can use this information to help you compare properties and provide you guidance on steps that can be taken to improve the energy efficiency of the property. Make sure that you consider these costs on your total budget if you decide to choose a home that needs improvements.

You should also check whether the home is in a High Radon Area. You can do this on the Environmental Protection Agency (EPA) Radon Risk Map found on their website *epa.ie* and also inquire as to whether the home has been tested for radon.

If the home was bought since 1 January, 2010, the price that was paid for it will be published on the Property Services Regulatory Authority's Residential Property Price Register website *propertypriceregister.ie*.

Buying the House

Once you have found a property that you like, any offer that you make on the property should be contingent on a property survey. In Ireland, the seller is under no obligation to disclose defects in a property, so you should get a survey of the property to find out if there are any defects before finalising the purchase. The Society of Chartered Surveyors Ireland (SCSI) is the professional body for chartered surveyors.

Go back to your lender to obtain a formal mortgage approval before you sign a contract for sale. Otherwise if you can't secure a mortgage for the property, you will lose your deposit and may face other penalties.

The two most common methods to buy and sell properties in Ireland are by private treaty sales and public auctions.

Private Treaty Sale

You can contact the seller or the seller's agent (usually an estate agent), to agree a purchase price. When there is an estate agent involved, you may be required to pay them a booking deposit once you have agreed to buy the property. Once you have paid the booking deposit, the legal process to buy the property may begin.

Obtain a formal mortgage approval from your mortgage provider. You will need to have mortgage protection insurance and home insurance. You can organise these with your mortgage provider but it is advisable to shop around.

Once your solicitor has checked the contract for sale, you will sign it and forward it to the sellers solicitors. At this point you have legally agreed to purchase the property. Once you have signed the contract you will need to pay a deposit (less any booking deposit), which is usually up to 10% of the purchase price. Be aware that the seller has only legally agreed to sell you their property once they have signed the contract.

Tips

- The booking deposit is refundable up to the signing of the contract for sale.

- Until the seller has signed the contract, they can still change their mind. This typically happens if they have been offered a higher price by another buyer.

Public Auction

A reserve figure is set for the property, usually by the seller or the auctioneer. The reserve figure is the value that the property must achieve. Anything below this and the property will be withdrawn from the market. But here's the catch – at all times during the auction the vendor (seller) can still withdraw the property from the market, even if it achieves the designated reserve amount. The vendor also has the right to sell the property before the auction.

There will be a designated date and time for the auction to take place. If you plan to bid on the property, then prior to the auction your solicitor should check the contract for sale for the property (issued by the seller's solicitor) and all title documents that are referred to in that contract. Once your solicitor has completed this, you can organise a survey of the property to ensure it is sound. You should also obtain a formal mortgage approval for the property.

If you are successful in bidding for the property, you will need to pay a deposit and sign the contract for sale. It is important to get home insurance as soon as possible.

Finalising the Purchase of the Property

To finalise the purchase of the property, you will need to sign the contract for sale. The contract for sale binds the parties to the completion of the sale. If you withdraw from the sale after this contract has been signed, you may lose your deposit.

- If you purchase your property at auction you must immediately sign the contract for sale.
- If you buy the property through private treaty your solicitor will check that the contract is in order before you sign it.

After signing the contract and before the completion date of the sale, your solicitor will carry out Requisitions on Title. This is where the solicitor raises general queries about the property with the seller's solicitor, such as, whether fixtures and fittings are included in the sale. Once these are finalised, a Deed of Conveyance is drafted by your solicitor and approved by the seller's solicitor.

Your solicitor will also carryout checks to ensure there are no judgements lying against the seller, e.g. bankruptcy and to ensure that there is nothing adverse attaching to the property, e.g. an outstanding mortgage.

Once the Deed of Conveyance is approved by the seller's solicitor, your solicitor will contact your mortgage provider to request the Loan Cheque – the remaining balance of the purchase price. It is paid to the seller's solicitor and all documentation and keys to the premises are handed over to your solicitor.

Stamp Duty

You will be required to pay a stamp duty tax on your new home. This is 1% of the total value of your new home up until €1 million, and 2% on any value above €2 million. Your solicitor will request this from you before the closing of the sale. The stamp duty is paid to the Revenue Commissioners, who place a stamp on the deeds (which name the owner of the property). Without this payment, the deeds cannot be registered.

Once the Sale Has Completed

Once the sale of the home has been completed, your deeds, showing the new ownership details and mortgage details (if applicable), must be registered with The Property Registration Authority (PRA).

Setting up Utilities

Once you have found a suitable place to live in, you need to set up your utilities. This book provides an overview including, what's available, and how to get them set up.

Tips

- Utility bills are regularly required as proof of residence (e.g. applying for your PPS Number, library etc…), so always keep your most recent utility bill.

Gas and Electricity

Modern homes may have solar panels installed. Some properties may have access to gas, but electricity is typically the main source of energy in Ireland. Both are quite expensive. Flats typically have pre-pay electricity set up in each flat.

Standard voltage in Ireland is 230V AC. Electricity is charged by the unit used and there are two different rates – daytime and night time. The day time rate is much more expensive than the night time rate. Consequently, if you are relying on electricity for heating, night store heaters can be more efficient.

The electricity services are distributed and maintained by the state owned Electrical Supply Board (ESB) *esb.ie*, however, they are not an electricity supplier. In order to connect your electricity services, you will need to contact one of the electricity suppliers listed below and become a new customer. Along with your personal details, meter reading, and bank details (if paying by direct debit) you will need to supply them with your ESB supplied Meter Point Reference Number (MPRN). The MPRN is an 11 digit number that identifies your properties unique connection. Your landlord should be able to supply you with this number.

Gas Only Supplier
- Flogas Natural Gas *flogas.ie*

Gas and Electricity Suppliers
- Bord Gáis Energy *bordgaisenergy.ie*
- Electric Ireland *electricireland.ie*
- Energia *energia.ie*
- SSE Airtricity *sseairtricity.com/ie*

Prepay Electricity Suppliers
- PrePayPower *prepaypower.ie*
- PINERGY *pinergy.ie*

Tips

- Use price comparison websites such as *bonkers.ie* and *switcher.ie* to help you find the best and cheapest supplier to meet your individual needs.
- You can set up a new account with any of the energy suppliers online or over the phone.

Water

The tap water in Ireland is safe to drink and is monitored by the local authorities to ensure a safe, quality supply. Water charges were introduced in 2014 and households began being billed for water in 2015. There is only one supplier, Irish Water. The Irish Water website *water.ie* has been set up to clearly explain the charges and how it works. Similar to other utility services, tenants are expected to sign up for an account with Irish Water.

Waste Removal

Rubbish collection (garbage / refuse) arrangements can vary area to area. Usually it is a private contractor to whom you will need to pay per rubbish bag or wheelie bin. Rubbish collection is usually done once a week. Rubbish and recycling is separated and your provider will tell you what goes in each bin. Glass has to be recycled separately (don't forget to remove the lid, as it's not glass).

To reduce your expenses, separate the recycling from the rubbish and take it to the public recycling bins in your local area. Find your nearest recycling centre on the website *repak.ie*. In general there is no charge at these civic amenities centres but it can be very inconvenient to have to store your recyclables and then take them to these bins, especially if you don't own a car. There are also landfill sites, but they charge fees.

If you are living in an apartment, then the waste is usually included in your rent and they will provide large waste skips for you to use.

Batteries and ink cartridges can be disposed in designated recycling locations, usually located in stationary stores and supermarkets.

Internet, Subscription TV and Phone Services

There are a number of types of internet services available in Ireland:

ADSL: Also known as broadband, this internet service is brought to you via the landline phone lines. Hence you will need to pay for line rental. Ireland is rolling out its Fibre Broadband network which will deliver greater internet speed.

Cable: Cable uses the same technology as ADSL but delivers it via cable TV. The advantages in choosing cable is that you won't have to pay line rental and, unlike ADSL, you won't suffer any slowdown in speeds during peak usage times because the line is not shared with anyone else.

Fixed Wireless Broadband: Fixed wireless broadband is an alternative to customers in rural areas where ADSL or cable is not available. A small transmitter in your local area broadcasts wireless signals that are picked up by a small antenna on your house, which channels the signal to a router or connection point inside the house.

Satellite broadband: Satellite is an option for those living in remote parts of Ireland with no cable, ADSL, fixed wireless or even mobile broadband service. The quality of the connection is more likely to be affected by adverse weather conditions and it is expensive to install.

Mobile Broadband: Mobile broadband allows you to access the internet via the 3G or 4G networks operated by mobile operators through either a USB dongle or modem plugged into your PC, laptop or mobile device, or using a WiFi Hotspot Device.

Combined Broadband Internet, Subscription TV, and Phone Bundles

If you want to access subscription pay TV, broadband internet, and landline phone services, then bundles can offer the best value for money and the ease of only having one monthly bill. However, be wary of price specials that offer a great introductory rate but then increase after a short period of time. Some of these deals are good value, but others could actually cost you more in the long run.

Providers:
- Sky *sky.com/ireland*
- Virgin Media *virginmedia.ie*
- Eircom *eir.ie*

Combined Broadband and Phone Service Bundles

Combined broadband and phone bundles are available for those of you who don't want to pay for subscription TV. In order to get broadband services you need to have a landline phone connection, so the deals usually include competitive call rates as well. If your phone line is not connected, your new provider can arrange to get this done.

Be wary of price specials that offer a great introductory rate but then increase after a short period of time. Some of these deals are good value but others could actually cost your more in the long run. You should also consider and compare the internet speeds. Fibre optic is available in many areas. Your supplier of choice will be able to advise you if you can access it.

Providers:
- Vodafone *vodafone.ie*
- Pure Telecom *puretelecom.ie*
- Magnet *magnet.ie*
- Sky *sky.com/ireland*
- Virgin Media *virginmedia.ie*
- Eircom *eir.ie*
- Imagine *imagine.ie*
- Digiweb *digiweb.co.uk*

Satellite Internet Providers

For those living in remote areas, there are also satellite broadband suppliers.

Providers:
- Q SAT *qsat.ie*
- onwave *onwave.ie*

Mobile Broadband

You can access mobile broadband services via a stick / dongle device, tethering your mobile phone or using a WiFi Hotspot Device.

Stick / Dongle: There are a number of companies that can provide you a stick / dongle style internet connection for your computer. Alternately, you could also get a mobile phone plan that includes data and connect your phone to your computer to access the internet. The data plans for dongles and mobile phones can be quite limited, but shop around as there are some good deals to be had.

Tethering: You can use your mobile phone internet plan by connecting your phone to your device using its USB charger cord. You typically need to go into your mobile phone settings and select tethering.

WiFi Hotspot Device: 3G or 4G WiFi hotspot devices are great because you can use them either plugged into your device or via Wifi. They can also provide a Wifi connection to more than one device at a time. There are lots of great deals, some even offering large data packages for the same price as a broadband service. Better yet, there is no waiting for it to be connected and you don't even need a phone connection. These devices are a good option for those living in flats or shared houses and need their own private internet connection. The provider that you purchase it from should be able to tell you whether or not your area has good coverage. They should also provide you with a guarantee that you can return the device if it does not work in the area you live.

Providers:
- Three Ireland (which has merged with O2) *three.ie*
- emobile *emobile.ie*
- Meteor *meteor.ie*
- Vodafone Ireland *vodafone.ie*

Mobile Phone Services

It can be tricky to get on a mobile phone plan if you are new to Ireland, as they usually like you to have been living there in the previous 6 months. However, this can depend on how 'flexible' the person signing you up is. You may also be able to get around this by paying a refundable deposit (usually after six months of service). If this is a problem, then you can just get a prepaid service. In some cases this may actually be the same price as a plan or even cheaper.

Providers:
- Three Ireland (which has merged with O2) *three.ie*
- emobile *emobile.ie*
- Meteor *meteor.ie*
- Vodafone Ireland *vodafone.ie*
- Tesco *tescomobile.ie*

Tips

- Use price comparison websites such as Bonkers *bonkers.ie* and Switcher *switcher.ie* to help you find the best and cheapest deal to meet your individual needs.

TV Services

Subscription Pay TV Service Providers

If you only want subscription TV services, Virgin Media and Sky offer a stand alone subscription TV service. Netflix is also available in Ireland.

Providers:
- Netflix *netflix.com/ie*
- Sky *sky.com/ireland*
- Virgin Media *virginmedia.ie*

Accessing Free TV

I found the entire TV system in Ireland quite confusing. The free Irish TV is quite limited and has only a handful of channels. The other option is paid TV, but if you are on a small budget this can be expensive. However, you can get more free TV channels by accessing the UK's free TV. I have outlined below how you can gain access to both of these free TV options.

How to Access the Free Irish TV

Raidió Teilifís Éireann (RTÉ) is the National Public Broadcaster for Ireland. They produce programs and broadcast them on television, radio and the Internet. RTÉ channels also show mainstream TV shows from around the world and their website *rte.ie* provides an RTÉ Player service which enables you to catch up on shows that you have missed.

Ireland no longer broadcasts analogue TV as it has been replaced with a digital signal. The free digital service that provides this RTÉ broadcast is called Saorview, which it is owned and managed by RTÉ. If you have an HD TV, you can simply receive the digital Saorview broadcast by connecting it to a TV aerial or rabbit ears. If you have an old TV that is not capable of digital TV, then you will need to purchase a Saorview Set Top Box.

How to Access the Free UK Channels in Ireland

With the right equipment you can also access the UK's free digital television service.

What is Free to Air, Freesat and Freeview?

You may hear these terms bandied around, but most people don't understand the difference. These services all play the same free UK channels; however they use a different type of receiver.

Free-to-Air: Is the free UK TV channels that can be received using an ITV/BBC patented satellite receiver and a satellite dish. (See option 1 and 2 below).

Freesat: Is the free UK TV channels that can be received using a generic satellite receiver and a satellite dish. (See option 3 and 4 below).

Freeview: This broadcast can be accessed via a TV aerial, but only in a few Irish coastal locations (and only if you have the aerial in the right spot).

Option 1: How to Access UK Free to Air Using an Old TV That Cannot Receive a Digital Signal

If you have an old TV that does not receive digital TV, then you can purchase a Saorview *Combi* Set Top Box (note: this is different to the Saorview Set Top Box as discussed above). This will enable you to receive both the Free to Air UK channels and the digital Saorview RTÉ channels. However, in order to access the Free to Air UK channels, it needs to be used in conjunction with a satellite dish.

Option 2: How to Access UK Free to Air Using a HD TV

You can use your normal TV aerial or rabbit ears to access the free Irish TV through the digital Saorview service.

To get the free UK channels, you need to purchase a Free to Air satellite receiver. It needs to be used in conjunction with a satellite dish. These two items can be bought together as a package.

Option 3: How to Access UK Freesat Using a HD TV

You can use your normal TV aerial or rabbit ears to access the free Irish TV through the free digital Saorview service.

To get the free UK channels, you need to purchase a Freesat box satellite receiver. It needs to be used in conjunction with a satellite dish. These two items can usually be bought together as a package.

Option 4: How to Access UK Freesat Using a Skybox

If you end your subscription with Sky, or have an old Skybox lying around, you can use it as a Freesat box. You will also need to have a satellite dish set up to receive the signal.

Accessing Freesat using a Skybox or Skybox+
1. Pull out your Sky card.
2. Pull out the power lead.
3. Wait a minute, then plug it back in and allow it to boot itself back up (this can take a few minutes).
4. Go to your channels list and all the free UK TV channels should come up.

Accessing Freesat Using a Skybox+HD Box
These boxes are a little bit trickier. Sky must have caught on that people were using their old Sky boxes in this manner, because they have programed it so that you cannot access the channel 4's, which broadcast many of the popular TV shows. In order to

'unlock' these channels you will need to purchase a Freesat card. Unfortunately these are not sold in Ireland, but if you know someone in the UK then get them to purchase one for you and post it over. If you don't know anyone in the UK, then there are people selling them on second hand websites in Ireland such as *adverts.ie, donedeal.ie* and *gumtree.ie*. But be careful of buying it this way as it comes with some risks. Just be sure to check with the seller that it works in a Skybox+HD and unlocks the channel 4's.

There are still some down sides – like you can't set the order of the channels. But to get around this you can use the 'favourites' function to store the channels that you like to watch and can access so you don't have to wade through the entire list of channels which includes those that you can't get. Be aware that you will also lose the functions that only Sky supports such as the record feature, freeze and rewind and access to the hard drive.

Option 5: You Are Completely Confused and out of Your Depth

Don't worry, there are lots of private TV services that can come out and install the equipment you need to access free UK TV.

Recommendations / Disclaimer: *I am not a TV professional. If you are going to try setting it up on your own then I definitely recommend that you discuss your needs with a professional. You need to ensure that you buy the right equipment and there are pros and cons that need to be considered before deciding on whether to go with the Free to Air or the Freesat box.*

Irish TV Licence

In Ireland, any home with a TV is expected to pay an annual TV licence. The bulk of this fee goes towards funding the free Irish TV, RTÉ. Even if you don't watch RTÉ, you are still are still required to pay for this licence if you own a TV or equipment capable of receiving a television signal. The Irish TV licence is managed by An Post, the Irish Postal Service. Be aware that failure to pay your TV licence can lead to a fine and a court conviction. Register for your TV license on the An Post website *anpost.ie*.

7 SHOPPING

Grocery Shopping

Unfamiliar shops, brands, and products make the relatively simple task of grocery shopping a real challenge. This guide will provide you an overview of what are available in Ireland and what to expect.

The range of supermarkets and their range of stock is much more limited in Ireland than you may expect to find in e.g. the UK, USA and Australia. They are generally quite small in size but in the suburban areas they have much larger superstores.

You will need to pack your own groceries, which can be frustrating if you are used to being in a country where supermarkets pack them for you! Sometimes there will be a person raising funds for a charity assisting you to pack – so you will be obliged to put some coins into their fundraising bucket.

Tips

- Cream cheese is sold as 'soft cheese'.
- Risoni is sold as 'orzo'.
- Flour used for bread making is sold as 'strong flour'.
- Ireland passed a plastic bag levy in 2002. So unless you want to pay 15 cents for a bag, then remember to bring your own.

Supermarket Opening hours

Many supermarkets are open 24/7 or have long opening hours like 08:00am – 10.00pm everyday. You can access individual store opening times on their websites.

Sale of Alcohol Laws in Ireland

Liquor is sold in supermarkets, however, off-licence sales of alcohol is only permitted between the hours of 10.30am and 10.00pm on weekdays and 12.30pm to 10.00pm on Sundays or St Patricks Day. Sales are not permitted on Good Friday or Christmas Day. This does not affect supermarket opening hours as they just block access to their alcoholic products outside of the permitted times.

Supermarkets in Ireland

Aldi

German based chain, very similar to Lidl.

- **Products:** Limited range, with a focus on staple items and a 'no-frills' approach to store layout. Mostly stock their own brand; however, they stock more branded products than Lidl. Similar to Lidl, in addition to its standard items Aldi has weekly special offers. Some of them are more expensive products such as electronics, tools, appliances, computers, through to cheap clothing, toys, flowers and gifts. Specials have strict limits on quantities and are available for one week or until they run out. You can sign up to their email newsletters to get an early preview of the specials.
- **Trolleys:** In order to use the trolleys, you will need to purchase a special Aldi token to insert into the trolley to unlock it from the other trolleys. If you are not a regular customer then this can be very annoying when compared with other supermarkets that only require you to use a €1 coin. However, the stores provide large and small baskets that can be used without a token.
- **Payment types:** Cash. In Ireland they accept debit cards and also Visa / MasterCard with no additional charge.

- **Customer loyalty scheme:** No.
- **Online shopping:** No.
- **Website:** *aldi.ie*

Dunnes Stores

Small Irish based retail chain. Not all of the stores contain a supermarket, so check their website for locations. It is not always obvious that the store contains a supermarket. Usually the supermarket department is down in the basement or the back of the store – so you usually have to walk through their clothing department to get to it.

- **Products:** Dunnes has a reasonable selection of products to choose from. They also stock their own branded products. The stores usually contain clothing, bedding and home wares but each store can vary what they sell, so check their website first to avoid disappointment.
- **Trolleys:** In order to use a trolley, you will need to insert a €1 coin to unlock it. The stores also provide small baskets that can be used without a token.
- **Payment types:** Cash, debit cards and Visa / MasterCard with no additional charge.
- **Customer loyalty scheme:** Yes, called VALUEclub.
- **Online shopping:** Not for their grocery department.
- **Website:** *dunnesstores.com*

Eurospar

Dutch multinational retail chain. Small convenience style supermarkets.

- **Products:** A small selection of branded products.
- **Trolleys:** In order to use a trolley, you will need to insert a €1 coin to unlock it. The stores also provide small baskets that can be used without a token.
- **Payment types:** Cash, debit cards and Visa / MasterCard with no additional charge.
- **Customer loyalty scheme:** Yes, called SuperEasy Rewards.
- **Online shopping:** No.

- **Website:** *eurospar.ie*

Lidl

German based chain, very similar to Aldi.

- **Products:** Limited range, with a focus on staple items and a 'no-frills' approach to store layout. They stock their own products as well as branded products. Similar to Aldi, in addition to its standard items Lidl has weekly special offers, some of them on more expensive products such as electronics, tools, appliances, computers, through to cheap clothing, toys, flowers and gifts. Specials have strict limits on quantities, and are available for one week or until they run out. You can sign up to their email newsletters to get an early preview of the specials.
- **Trolleys:** In order to use a trolley, you will need to insert a €1 coin to unlock it. The stores also provide small baskets that can be used without a token.
- **Payment types:** Cash, debit cards and Visa / MasterCard with no additional charge.
- **Customer loyalty scheme:** No.
- **Online shopping:** No.
- **Website:** *lidl.ie*

Marks & Spencer (AKA M&S)

UK based retail chain. Not all of the stores contain a supermarket, so be sure to check their website for locations. It is not always obvious that the store contains a supermarket as often the supermarket part is in back of the store.

- **Products:** Known as a luxury food store, they also sell a large range of pre-prepared food. They also sell niche items that you may not find in other stores.
- **Trolleys:** In order to use a trolley, you will need to insert a €1 coin to unlock it. The stores also provide small baskets that can be used without a token.
- **Payment types:** Cash, debit cards and Visa / MasterCard with no additional charge.
- **Customer loyalty scheme:** No.

- **Online shopping:** Yes, but you must collect it in store, they do not home deliver groceries.
- **Website:** *marksandspencer.ie*

Supervalu

Irish based supermarket chain.

- **Products:** Supervalu stock their own brand of products as well as branded products.
- **Trolleys:** In order to use a trolley, you will need to insert a €1 coin to unlock it. The stores also provide small baskets that can be used without a token.
- **Payment types:** Cash, debit cards and Visa / MasterCard with no additional charge.
- **Customer loyalty scheme:** Yes, called Real Rewards.
- **Online shopping:** Yes.
- **Website:** *supervalu.ie*

Tesco

UK based chain store.

- **Products:** Tesco has a broader selection of products to choose from. They stock their own brand of products alongside branded products. Some of the larger stores also sell their cheap clothing range and home wares, electronics, garden items etc…
- **Trolleys:** In order to use a trolley, you will need to insert a €1 coin to unlock it. The stores also provide small baskets that can be used without a token.
- **Payment types:** Cash, debit cards and Visa / MasterCard with no additional charge.
- **Customer loyalty scheme:** Yes, called Clubcard. You can collect points not only with your grocery shopping, but also at other Tesco businesses and business partners.
- **Online shopping:** Yes.
- **Website:** *tesco.ie*

Shopping for Household Essentials

If you have had to pay the high cost of getting your personal effects shipped to Ireland, then you probably got rid of a lot of things and now need some basic household essentials. But when you arrive in Ireland you will probably have no idea which shops to visit for basic items such as linens, kitchenware, and electrical. Furthermore you'll have no idea which are the best luxury shops or the budget shops. This guide will provide you an overview of the main department stores in Ireland and what to expect from them.

Typical Opening Hours

Shops in Ireland may open whenever they want, including Sundays and public holidays, but they are typically open:

- Monday, Tuesday, Wednesday, Friday, Saturday: 8:00/9:00/10:00 – 17:00/18:00/19:00
- Thursday: 8:00/9:00/10:00 – 20:00/21:00/22:00
- Sunday: 9:00/10:00/11:00 – 17:00/18:00/19:00

Large shopping centres and out of town suburban centres are typically open longer hours everyday:

- Weekdays 09:00 – 21:00/22:00
- Saturdays 09:00 – 19:00
- Sundays 10:00 – 19:00

In the two weeks running up to Christmas, it is common for many shops to have extended opening hours. Some may operate 24 hours until midnight on Christmas Eve.

Most shops in smaller towns and villages don't open on Sundays. Shops are usually closed on Christmas Day, though most are open on all other holidays.

Shopping for Bedding in Ireland

Ireland shares the same bed sizing as the UK. For those of you from countries that use the bed size 'Queen' and 'King' – the Irish King size is similar (though slightly smaller) to a 'Queen', and the 'Super King' is similar (though slightly smaller) to the 'King'.

Sheets are usually sold singularly (flat or fitted). Sheets are not commonly sold in sets (i.e. flat and fitted sheet and pillowcases in one package).

Pillowcases are usually sold in pairs. The opening / closure of the case is usually a pocket inside the open end to enclose the pillow. In other countries the square / continental pillow is often called a "European sized pillow".

Bed types and sizes that you might expect:

- *Single Bed:* 90cm x 190cm; 35in x 75in.
- *Double Bed:* 135cm x 190cm; 53in x 75in.
- *King Bed:* 150cm x 200cm; 59in x 79in.
- *Super King Bed:* 180cm x 200cm; 71in x 79in.

Tips

- An Oxford pillowcase is one that has an extended material edging / valance trim.
- When purchasing a duvet cover, be aware that some of the more expensive brands sometimes sell their pillow cases separately, making this an additional cost to consider when comparing prices.
- In the higher quality range of sheets, there is usually the option to purchase 'deep fitted' sheets to accommodate for modern extra thick mattresses.

Department Stores

What is Click & Collect?

A free service where you can purchase your product of choice online and then choose which store you wish to collect it from.

Price Range:

€€€€ = Expensive
€€€ = Pricey
€€ = Moderate
€ = Cheap

Upmarket Department Stores

Arnotts

A very large and rather confusingly laid out department store in Dublin where you will find a wide range of quality branded products, but for a price. They sell a wide range of items including clothing, beauty, furniture and accessories, homeware, home appliances, televisions and audio, computers and cameras.

- **Price Range:** €€€
- **Online Shopping:** Yes
- **Click & Collect:** Yes
- **Loyalty Card:** Yes
- **Website:** *arnotts.ie*

Brown Thomas

An Irish chain of department stores specialising in high end luxury goods. This store will suit those of you not fazed at paying high prices for upmarket products.

- **Price Range:** €€€€
- **Online Shopping:** Yes
- **Click & Collect:** Yes
- **Loyalty Card:** Yes
- **Website:** *brownthomas.com*

Debenhams

Stocks a range of quality products that provides pricey through to more moderately priced choices. They stock a wide range of products including beauty, clothing, furniture and accessories, homeware, home appliances, televisions and audio, computers and cameras.

- **Price Range:** €€€-€€
- **Online Shopping:** Yes
- **Click & Collect:** Yes
- **Loyalty Card:** Yes
- **Website:** *debenhams.ie*

House of Fraser

Located in the Dublin suburb of Dundrum only. British department store that has a nice range of products, but a bit on the pricey side. They stock fashion, beauty, homeware and accessories.

- **Price Range:** €€€
- **Online Shopping:** Yes
- **Click & Collect:** Yes
- **Loyalty Card:** Yes
- **Website:** *houseoffraser.co.uk*

Affordable / Mid-Range Department Stores

Dunnes

A good store to purchase affordable clothing, beauty products, kitchen and homeware. Some of the stores also have a Dunnes grocery department. The stores also have an open layout, making it easy to find your way around.

- **Price Range:** €€
- **Online Shopping:** Yes
- **Click & Collect:** Yes
- **Loyalty Card:** Yes
- **Website:** *dunnesstores.com*

Marks & Spencers (AKA M&S)

A good range of affordable clothing, beauty products, furniture, homeware and a limited range of kitchenware. Some of the stores also have an M&S grocery department.

- **Price Range:** €€
- **Online Shopping:** Yes
- **Click & Collect:** Yes
- **Loyalty Card:** Yes
- **Website:** marksandspencer.ie

Budget Department Stores

Argos

An interesting store concept as they have no goods on display.

Instead, they have a huge catalogue that you can view via their telephone book sized catalogues or online. You then order the item/s you want online, choosing the store that you wish to collect it from, or in store (be aware that sometimes the stock may not be available at the store that you want to collect it from). You pay for your items in store, then you will be given a ticketed number to collect it. They stock everything from homeware, home appliances, televisions and audio, computers, cameras as well as furniture.

- **Price Range:** € - €€
- **Online Shopping:** Yes
- **Home Delivery:** Only for large items.
- **Click & Collect:** Yes
- **Loyalty Card:** No
- **Website:** *argos.ie*

Guineys (AKA Michael Guineys)

Basic products, cheap prices, they sell homeware. The quality at these stores can really vary, and sometimes the stores are not in the best of order. However, bargains, especially on linens, are to be had if you are on a tight budget.

- **Price Range:** €
- **Online Shopping:** Yes
- **Click & Collect:** No
- **Loyalty Card:** No
- **Website:** *guineys.ie*

Ikea

If you prefer bed and bathroom linens of a higher quality, then this is not the place to get them. However, this is a great place to go if you want to completely kit out your new home in one budget friendly shopping trip. They sell Scandinavian style furniture, accessories and homeware. Beware - once you enter the store, you'll be in there for a while, fun for some, a nightmare for others. You are made to follow a path through the entire store just to get to the exit.

For large items, you need to write down the code found on the display furniture and then find and collect them from the warehouse shelves (located at the end of your journey, just before the cashiers). They have an assistant in each section that can check whether the item is in stock. One of the most frustrating things about Ikea is that they are frequently out of stock. If you already know what you want prior to visiting (their website showcases all of their items), then check their stocks by ringing them or checking online to avoid disappointment.

Just be careful that what you buy actually fits in your car! They do offer delivery services, but at a cost to you. Their furniture items require assembly, but for a fee they can arrange for someone to come to your home and assemble it for you.

- **Price range:** €
- **Online Shopping:** No
- **Click & Collect:** No, but for a fee they will find and collect the items you want and have them ready for you at an agreed time at the tills ready for payment.
- **Home Delivery:** Yes
- **Loyalty Card:** No
- **Website:** *ikea.com/ie/en/*

Penneys (AKA Primark)

Ireland's beloved budget retailer stock clothing, beauty products, and a small range of cheap bed, bath and kitchen linens. When you see the cheap prices, it's easy to get carried away and buy things you do not need.

- **Price Range:** €
- **Home Delivery:** No
- **Click & Collect:** No
- **Loyalty Card:** No
- **Website:** *primark.com/en-ie/homepage*

TK Maxx (AKA TJ Maxx)

An outlet style store which stock mostly clothes and a small range of homewares and accessories. Bargains can be had if you are in the store at the right time, however, stock varies so you may not always find what you are after.

- **Price Range:** €€-€
- **Online Shopping:** No

- **Click & Collect:** No
- **Loyalty Card:** No
- **Website:** *tkmaxx.ie*

Online Department Stores

What You Need to Know When Shopping Online in Ireland

When purchasing goods online from EU countries, Irish Value Added Taxes (VAT) will be charged to your purchases. This usually occurs at the checkout stage once you have identified Ireland as your shipping destination (as EU countries have varying VAT rates).

When purchasing items online from a non-EU website, they won't charge the Irish VAT, but they may charge their local VAT. Because the Irish VAT is so high, it may make the online purchase price appear like an irresistible bargain when you see it without VAT. However, don't think that you are going avoid paying the Irish VAT on your purchase. The Irish Post Office, An Post, will apply the Irish VAT to your purchase and collect it from you when they deliver your goods. So what may seem like a bargain may actually end up being an expensive purchase once you add on the rather steep Irish VAT charges.

Amazon

Irish residents use the UK site, so be aware that shipping costs can apply. Unfortunately there are a lot of retailers that won't ship to Ireland. Keep in mind that the prices are in pounds. When you get to the payment part of your order it will be converted into Euro, however, be aware that VAT is higher in Ireland so this will also be added on to your purchase during the payment process.

- **Price range:** € - €€€€
- **Website:** amazon.co.uk

Littlewoods

An Irish online only retailer. A good range of products, including clothing, beauty, furniture and accessories, homeware, home appliances, televisions and audio, computers and cameras. Littlewoods can be on the pricey side.

- **Price range:** €€€
- **Website:** *littlewoodsireland.ie*

Specialty Electrical Stores

If purchasing electrical goods online, don't forget to ensure that it has the correct plug – otherwise, be prepared to buy an adaptor for it. There will also be a number of locally owned electrical stores as well, but these are the main chain stores:

Currys

Has a range of kitchen and home appliances, televisions and audio, computers and cameras. Some of the smaller stores only sell electronics.

- **Price Range:** €€€
- **Online Shopping:** Yes
- **Click & Collect:** Yes
- **Loyalty Card:** No
- **Website:** *currys.ie*

D.I.D Electrical

Has a range of kitchen and home appliances, televisions and audio, computers and cameras.

- **Price Range:** €€€
- **Online Shopping:** No
- **Click & Collect:** No
- **Loyalty Card:** No
- **Website:** *did.ie*

Expert

Has a range of kitchen and home appliances, televisions and audio, computers and cameras.

- **Price Range:** €€€
- **Online Shopping:** No
- **Click & Collect:** No
- **Loyalty Card:** No
- **Website:** *expert.ie*

Harvey Norman

Is an Australian-based chain that has a range of kitchen and home appliances, televisions and audio, computers, cameras as well as furniture.

- **Price Range:** €€€
- **Online Shopping:** Yes
- **Click & Collect:** Yes
- **Loyalty Card:** No
- **Website:** *harveynorman.ie*

Power City

Has a range of kitchen and home appliances, televisions and audio, computers and cameras.

- **Price Range:** €€€
- **Online Shopping:** No ·
- **Click & Collect:** No
- **Loyalty Card:** No
- **Website:** *powercity.ie*

Buying Second Hand

Second Hand Stores

There are lots of second hand furniture stores and charity shops. A quick online search will find your local retailers. There are also plenty of antique stores for those of you with a bit more money and looking for something unique.

Buying Second Hand Online

People tend to overprice their wares, so be sure to first check the recommended retail price (RRP) of similar new items before making an offer. The sites available offer similar services.

- *Adverts.ie*
- *Donedeal.ie*
- *Gumtree.ie*

Tips

- Be very careful if you are buying or selling items online.

There are a lot of scams. Go with your gut and always be weary of deals that seem too good to be true. If your selling something, scammers will usually offer you your asking price or even more, and then ask you to post it to them or their 'relative' at another location (usually overseas). They tell you to send them a PayPal invoice (it's usually PayPal, but it can be other payment services).

- There are people that offer to buy your item, then just don't show up and ones that seem to enjoy leading you on, always changing the collection arrangements, but never being able to make it – they are time wasters.
- Make sure you check their buyers / sellers feedback scores and reviews. Also, be wary of communication in broken English and anyone offering more than you have asked for.
- It's safer to sell in person and receive cash. Always meet them in a safe public place, and take a friend for support. If you have to go alone, then be sure to tell someone where you are going.

8 WORK

Public Holidays

Public Holiday Dates

There are nine public holidays per year in Ireland.

- *1 January New Year's Day:* Most also take time off work for New Year's Eve.
- *17 March Saint Patrick's Day.*
- *Easter Monday*:* Also coincides with the commemoration of the Easter Rising.
- *The first Monday in May*
- *The first Monday in June:* Previously observed as Whit Monday until 1973.
- *The first Monday in August*
- *The last Monday in October*
- *25 December Christmas Day:* Most start Christmas celebrations on Christmas Eve, including taking time off work.
- *26 December St. Stephen's Day (AKA Boxing day):* Celebrating the feast day of Saint Stephen.

*Good Friday is not a public holiday, while some schools and businesses close on that day you have no automatic entitlement to time off work.

Public Holiday Business Opening Hours

On these days, most businesses and schools close. However, many of the larger chain and department stores in the cities usually stay open, except for Christmas day.

Public Holiday Sale of Alcohol Laws

The sale of alcohol is only permitted between the hours of 10.30am and 10.00pm on St Patrick's Day. Sales are not permitted on Good Friday or Christmas Day. This does not affect supermarket opening hours on these days as they just block access to their alcoholic products outside of these permitted times.

Public Transport on Irish Public Holidays

Public transport still operates, but on restricted schedules.

Public Holiday Employment Rules in Ireland

Most employees are entitled to paid leave on public holidays and they receive one of the following:

- A paid day off.
- An additional day of annual leave.
- An additional days pay.
- A paid day off within a month of the public holiday.

If the public holiday falls on a weekend, you do not have the automatic entitlement to have the next working day off. It is up to your employer whether you need to work that day. They can provide you with any of the above four options.

Part-time employees who have not worked for their employer at least 40 hours in total in the 5 weeks before the public holiday are not entitled to the holiday benefits.

What to Expect on St Patricks Day in Ireland

In the city areas, especially Dublin, it can become overcrowded with tourists flying in to experience the true St Patrick day. Most main centres put on parades and festivals for the public, however, while tourists and young folk flock to the cities to party hard, the rest of Ireland tend to have a more family and community approach to the celebrations.

Off-licence sales of alcohol is only permitted between the hours of 10.00pm on St Patricks Day.

What to Expect over the Christmas Period in Ireland

Many businesses and workplaces close for the period from Christmas day until the working day that follows New Years day.

Employment Legislation and Rights

Disclaimer: *This article covers general information about finding a job in Ireland and does not take your individual circumstances into account. Please use it as a guide only.*

Ireland has minimum standard employment legislation in place to provide rights to all employees. Rights can vary between industries, but there are minimum standards in place. Below are excerpts of these standards.

Employment Contract

The employee must receive a written contract clearly outlining the terms and conditions of their employment that includes details of the following information:

- The title and nature of the work.
- Pay.
- Paid leave.
- Sick leave.
- Hours of work, including overtime.
- Pensions.
- Notice period that the employee is require to give and entitled to receive.
- Any collective agreements that directly affect the terms and conditions of the employment contract.

Pay

Employees must receive payslips which clearly detail gross pay and deductions.

The amount that you get paid is typically negotiated between you and your employer. However, in some sectors the rates of pay are set by Registered Employment Agreements (REAs) made by collective agreements.

Minimum Wage

Ireland has a National Minimum Wage Act which sets the minimum wage for trainees, employees under 18 years of age, and adult employees 18 years of age and over. This does not stop the employer from offering a higher wage, but ensures that they provide you a minimum. For more information about how these rates are calculated, see the *citizensinformation.ie* website.

Salaries

Like most European countries, incomes are less that you might expect in other countries such as the US and Australia. However, those with unique skills in high demand may find themselves being offered high salaries.

Holidays

Annual Leave

All employees that have worked at least 1365 hours per year are entitled to a minimum of four weeks paid holiday per year. This includes full time, part time, temporary, or casual employees.

Public Holidays

Most employees are entitled to paid leave on public holidays and they receive one of the following:
- A paid day off.
- An additional day of annual leave.
- An additional days pay.
- A paid day off within a month of the public holiday.

If the public holiday falls on a weekend, you do not have the automatic entitlement to have the next working day off. It is up to your employer whether you need to work that day. They can provide you with any of the above four options.

Part-time employees who have not worked for their employer at least 40 hours in total in the 5 weeks before the public holiday are not entitled to the holiday benefits.

Other Leave

Sick Leave

Employees have no right to paid sick leave under the employment laws. It is up to the employer to decide on their own sick leave policy and they must provide you with the terms of this in your employment contract.

Maternity Leave

All female employees are entitled to maternity leave if they become pregnant whilst in employment. Ireland provides 26 weeks of maternity leave benefits as well as 16 weeks of additional unpaid maternity leave. At least 2 weeks of leave must be taken before the expected birth date and at least 4 weeks after.

The maternity benefit will only be paid if you have made sufficient PRSI contributions (social insurance) to be eligible. Applications for the benefit should be made at least six weeks before maternity leave is due to start, or 12 weeks if self-employed. The Department of Social Protection is responsible for issuing the Maternity Benefit.

Learn more about the Irish Maternity benefit from the Irish Department of Social Protection website *welfare.ie*.

Paternity Leave

From September 2016, fathers have the option to apply for two weeks' paid paternity leave following the birth of their child. The new statutory paternity leave will be paid at the same rate as maternity benefit, and based on the same PRSI contribution requirements.

Typical Irish Working Day

The Irish generally have a good work life balance. Days of work are typically Monday to Friday, 9am to 5.30pm. Unless of course you work in an industry that requires you to work outside of these times. Those in high level roles may be expected to work extended hours.

Employees are entitled to take a 15 minute break after working 4.5 hours, but are not entitled to be paid for these breaks. However, many employers do pay staff for this time. If employees work more than 6 hours, then they would typically get a one hour unpaid lunch break.

The average working week is 39 hours. The legal maximum working week is 48 hours. Those that work less than 5 days a week are considered 'part time'.

Those expected to work on Sundays are required to be compensated by being paid at a higher rate.

Tips

To learn more about Ireland's employment legislation and rights, go to:

* *citizensinformation.ie*
* *workplacerelations.ie*

How to Find a Job

First of all, if you are not from the European Economic Area (EEA), then it's important that you have the right visa or work permit before applying for work.

To be successful, you will need a good level of spoken and written English. Being fluent in another language can also be a real advantage for work with multinational companies. Those with skills in the technology, science, finance, HR, and health areas are in high demand.

If your trade or profession requires registration, then you should get in contact with the relevant body as soon as possible to have your qualifications assessed. You may need to undertake an examination or further training to meet the expected skills and qualifications.

If you are seeking a job that requires qualifications, you will need to provide proof. You may be asked to provide a qualification recognition certificate in order to provide evidence that your credentials are formally recognised in Ireland. To apply for this certificate, contact Qualifications Recognition Ireland. Learn more at their website *qqi.ie*. Degrees from most Western countries are usually considered equivalent to Irish qualifications.

Tips

- Prepare your CV. It should include your personal contact details, educational and employment history, details about your relevant skills and arrange for references.
- Once you have been offered a job, you will need to apply for an Irish PPS number. You will also need to have an Irish bank account to be paid into.

Avenues For Finding Work in Ireland

Irish Recruitment Agencies

Recruitment agencies can be a great resource for you to tap into when carrying out your job hunt. They actively recruit skilled workers in the high demand industries.

However, you may find it very difficult to get any response from the job agencies before you arrive in Ireland. If you don't have much luck, it's best to contact them once you arrive in Ireland. This will show that you are serious and have made the move and your not just thinking about it. Once they see that you have an Irish phone number and address, you will hopefully see more interest from recruiters.

Unfortunately recruitment agencies receive vast amounts of enquiries so may not be very responsive. In that case, it would be best for you to register with several recruitment agencies to increase your chances of success. However, it is not recommended that you apply for the same job through more than one agency.

There are a large number of recruitment agencies throughout Ireland. Some focus on specific industries, but others are broader. A good place to start your search would be using the agency directory and agency list on the National Recruitment Federation (NRF) website, *nrf.ie*. The NRF is a voluntary organisation that grants membership to recruitment agencies that meet their criteria of excellence.

Tips

- In Ireland, recruitment agencies cannot charge for their services.

Irish Job Websites

There are an ever growing number of job websites offering a variety of employment opportunities. As well as jobs, they also provide lots of great advice about tailoring your cover letter and CV for the Irish market as well as interview tips. Employers are increasingly choosing to advertise online over the traditional newspapers.

All Sectors

- *bestjobs.ie*
- *careerbuilder.ie*
- *careerjet.ie*
- *dublinwork.com*
- *frsrecruitment.com*
- *graftonrecruitment.com*
- *hays.ie*
- *headhunt.ie*
- *ie.indeed.com*
- *irishjobs.ie*
- *irishtimes.com*
- *jobs.ie*
- *jobsguideireland.com*
- *jobs.movetodublin.com*
- *jobsireland.ie*
- *jobsearch.ie*
- *manpower.ie*
- *monster.ie*
- *osborne.ie*
- *reedglobal.com*
- *recruitireland.com*

Construction
- *construction-jobs.ie*

Education
- *educationposts.ie*

Finance
- *financejobs.ie*

Graduates
- *gradireland.com*

Health
- *cplhealthcare.com*
- *jackiebrownmedical.ie*

Hospitality
- *hoteljobs.ie*

IT

- *glassdoor.com*
- *hookhead.com*
- *makeitinireland.com*

Language Jobs
- *toplanguagejobs.ie*
- *europelanguagejobs.com*

Media & Marketing
- *prosperity.ie*

Nonprofit
- *activelink.ie*

Public sector
- *publicjobs.ie*

Tips

- If you don't have access to the internet, then you can use it for free on the public computers at your local Irish library.

Using Social Media to Find Work in Ireland

Social Media like Twitter, Facebook, Google+, and LinkedIn have become a popular way for people to share and promote job opportunities amongst like minded people. If you work in a particular industry that uses social media in this way, then try following people in key roles to learn more about any opportunities that may be available. Make sure that you spend time developing your LinkedIn profile as it is a popular website in Ireland and many businesses use it to headhunt for key roles.

Tips

- Create different social media accounts to keep your professional and personal profiles separate.

Job Advertisements in Irish Newspapers

Although much of the job advertising is done via job websites, there are still many jobs advertised in the Irish newspapers. The Irish Times both publishes jobs and host their own web based job search on their website *irishtimes.com.*

The Irish Independent, which also publishes the Sunday Independent, and The Evening Herald publish job advertisements and on their websites, their online job search links to the *irishjobs.ie* website.

The local newspapers are also a good place to search for local jobs.

Tips

- Save money by accessing the newspapers for free at your local Irish Library.

Open Days and Recruitment Days in Ireland

Search the internet for open days, recruitment days or events that may be occurring in your area. It will give you the chance to

117

make connections and learn more about the different companies and their job opportunities. It could even lead to a job.

Tips

- Dress professionally and treat it like a job interview. These events are usually hosted by HR staff that may hold the key to you getting a job.
- Take along copies of your CV to handout. Make sure that they include your contact details.

Volunteering in Ireland

Struggling to get work? Then the next best step is to gain work experience by volunteering through Volunteer Ireland. Their website *volunteer.ie* posts volunteer opportunities from all over Ireland and also provides details about how to get the volunteer position that you're after.

Job Seeker Support Services

Government Funded Employment Services in Ireland

The Government contracts organisations to provide their employment services.

The central point for these services is the Local Employment Service Network (LESN). Their website *localemploymentservices.ie* will provide you the details of your nearest local centre.

These centres provide support to jobseekers including assistance with preparing a CV, finding a job, interview coaching, and also information on support available for starting your own business.

Employment for People from Immigrant Communities (EPIC) In Dublin

For immigrants living in Ireland, EPIC can provide support with preparing a CV and cover letter, advice on how to look for a job as well as interview skills. You can find EPIC on *facebook.com/EpicProgram*.

Irish Workplace Dress Code

Dress for success. Make a good first impression and show your respect by wearing professional attire at your job interviews.

Unless you are expected to wear a uniform, many Irish workplaces don't have official dress codes as it is usually implied. Even if there is a dress code, they can be quite generalised. The expected attire can vary from smart casual to professional, depending on the workplace culture. Once you start your new job, it would be safer to turn up in a professional outfit on your first day. This will make a good impression and avoid any possible embarrassment on your part. You can always tone it down the next day.

How to Become an Au Pair in Ireland

Becoming an Au Pair gives you the opportunity to live and work in a different country. It's a great way to experience a new culture and improve your English. Although there is no official Au Pair program in Ireland, it is still possible to become one.

Au Pair Mandatory Criteria

- You must be between 18-30 years old.
- You need to have a good working knowledge of English.
- Have no criminal record.
- Be in good health.
- Be willing to undertake first aid training prior to commencement.
- Be willing to commit to a family for a minimum of six months (although sometimes this can be negotiable). There are also summer Au Pair opportunities where the minimum stay is typically nine weeks.

Au Pair Working Conditions and Expectations

The working hours for an Au Pair in Ireland are not specified but generally 20 hours if you are on a student visa or approximately 35 hours per week. You can expect to be paid anywhere from €80 to €120 per week. There have been concerns raised in Ireland over whether Au Pairs should be receiving the legal minimum wage with a small deduction for room and board.

The free time and holidays for an Au Pair in Ireland are not specified, but it is recommended that Au Pairs receive two days free time per week and one weeks paid holidays for every six months worked. You may be expected to babysit on weekends.

Accommodation and Meals

'Au Pair' means on an equal footing and you should not be treated like a servant. The host family is expected to treat you as a member of their family. They must provide you with your own bedroom, three meals per day, and also free access to the family home.

Au Pair Job Duties

Au Pair duties include childcare and light housework. For example:
- Playing with children and assisting them with their homework.
- Preparing snacks and meals for the children.
- Dropping off and picking up children from school and/or child care.
- Light housework such as washing, ironing, vacuum, tidying.

Driving

Many families require the Au Pair to be able to drive in order to transport the children to school and appointments. If you are required to drive as an Au Pair in Ireland, you will need a full, valid driver's licence. If the family provides the Au Pair with a car for private use, it would be expected that the Au Pair pay for the petrol used.

Discuss with your host family what happens if you have a car accident, who pays, and have your agreements put in the contract.

Travel Costs

The Au Pair is liable for all costs, however, in some cases the host family may contribute to the cost if the Au Pair is travelling a long way.

Insurances

It is strongly recommended that Au Pairs obtain comprehensive travel insurance, which covers medical, accident, and liability costs. This would be at the Au Pair's own expense.

Non-EU citizens who have entered with a student visa must also have adequate private medical insurance.

Language Skills and Courses

An Au Pair in Ireland needs to have a working knowledge of English. Many take the opportunity to attend a language course or study while in Ireland, but this is not a requirement. Typically the Au Pair would bear the cost of the course, but there are cases where the host family may assist.

How to Become an Au Pair or Find an Au Pair in Ireland

Looking to become an Au Pair or wanting to host an Au Pair? There are a number of sites that can assist you. Some sites simply act as a platform for potential Au Pairs to meet host families; others are agencies that match Au Pairs with a family for a fee.

- Au Pair Ireland *aupairireland.ie*
- Au Pair in Ireland *aupairinireland.ie*
- Au Pair Agency *aupairagency.ie*
- S K Dublin *skdublin.ie*
- Au Pair Ireland *aupairireland.com*
- Cara International *carainternational.net*

Au Pair Visa Information

European Union (EU) / European Free Trade Association (EFTA)

EU and EFTA nationals do not require a work permit, but must register with local authorities (Garda) after arriving in Ireland.

Non EEU/EFTA

In order for non-EU nationals to become an au pair in Ireland, they are required to have a Work Permit. Some of the types of work permits that you may be able to apply for are:

- Student visa in Ireland.
- Working Holiday Maker program in Ireland.
- Work & Travel program in Ireland.

For information about obtaining a visa, visit the Irish Naturalisation and Immigration Service website *inis.gov.ie*.

Au Pair Scams

Be aware that there are a number of scams that people get caught up in. If the 'host family' asks you to hand over large sums of money for e.g. visas, then this is most likely a scam. Vice versa, 'Au Pairs' who request money from their host family prior to commencing is most likely a scam as the Au Pair is expected to pay for their own travel expenses.

Personal Public Service Number

What Is an Irish PPS Number?

A Personal Public Service number (PPSN) number is a unique number that government bodies use to identify you. You will need to give this number to your employer as soon as possible so that they can advise the Revenue Commissioners for your tax deductions. You may also need it when setting up a bank account or accessing public services.

When you are allocated your PPSN, you will be issued a Public Services Card. On the front of the card will be your name, photograph and signature, along with the card expiry date. The back of the card holds your PPS number and a card number. It also holds a magnetic stripe to enable social welfare payments such as pensions to be collected at post offices.

The PPS number will also give you access to Irish services such as:

- Social welfare

- Free Travel Pass
- Public health services
- Child immunisation
- Housing grants
- Driver licences

When can I apply for a PPS Number?

You cannot apply for a PPS number before you arrive in Ireland. You must be living in Ireland in order to apply.

As well evidence of an address, you will also need to show that you have a requirement for one, otherwise it won't be issued. For example, you will only be issued with a PPS number if you are about to commence employment. Looking for employment is not considered a requirement. Be aware that an employer requiring a PPS number as part of the application process is in breach of the legislation.

How Do I apply for a PPS Number?

You need to go to your local Department of Social Protection and complete an application form. Be prepared to line up! It can get pretty busy at these offices. Find your nearest office on their website *welfare.ie*.

If you are not Irish, you will need to provide the following documents:

- Non EU/EEA your current passport.
- EU/EEA current passport or national identity card.
- Proof of address, such as a household bill with your name on it. Proof of address can be difficult to provide if you have only just arrived in Ireland and are immediately commencing employment. In this case, your employer may apply on your behalf.

Do My Children Need a PPS Number?

When a child is born in Ireland, they are given a PPS number when their birth is registered with the General Register Office. In this case, they do not need to apply for one. However, if both parents live outside of the state, this will not automatically occur and you will still need to apply for one.

For children living in, but not born in Ireland the parent / guardian must apply for one. However, the parent / guardian must already have their own PPS number in order for the child to be registered and linked with them.

What Does the PPS Number Look Like?

Your PPS number will have seven numbers and will end in two letters, making up nine characters in total. Old PPS numbers are only eight characters as they only have one letter at the end.

I Have Lost My PPS Number, Where Can I Find It?

Your PPS number will be recorded on your tax documents, your payslip and any letter or cards that are issued from the social welfare office, medical payment scheme or tax office.

Changing My Listed Address

You must notify the Department of Social Protection of your change of address as they will update your record. You can do this by either calling or writing to them. You can access their contact details at the website *welfare.ie*.

Pay Related Social Insurance

Employers as well as employees over 16 years of age and under 66 pay compulsory contributions to Ireland's Social Insurance Fund. The contribution that you pay depends on your earnings and occupation and is called a Pay Related Social Insurance (PRSI) contribution.

As an employee, your PRSI contributions will be deducted from your wages by your employer and collected by the Irish Revenue Department under the Pay As You Earn (PAYE) system. PRSI is calculated on your reckonable pay which is basically your gross pay plus notional pay. In certain cases, if your income falls below a certain amount you do not have to pay a social insurance contribution, however, you will still be covered by social insurance because your employer must pay social insurance for you.

If you are self-employed, you pay Class S social insurance contributions directly to the Revenue Commissioners. From 2014 unearned income such as rents, investments, dividends, and interest on deposits and savings also became liable for PRSI. Once collected from you, Revenue Commissioners then pay this money into the Social Insurance Fund. The Social Insurance Fund is made up of two accounts:

- Current account: This account is managed by the Minister for Social Protection and consists of monies collected from people in employment. It is used to fund social insurance payments.
- Investment account: This account is managed by the Minister for Finance. This is a savings account.

PRSI Classes

There are currently 11 different PRSI classes - A, B, C, D, E, H, J, K, M, S and P. The social insurance payments to which you may become entitled depend on the PRSI class you are in.

Each PRSI class is divided into different subclasses, however, these subclasses do not affect your entitlements under the social insurance system. They only relate to the amount of PRSI which you or your employer must pay.

PRSI Contribution Week

The PRSI contribution week starts on 1 January each year. Your working week may not be the same as the PRSI contribution week.

Rates

The amount of PRSI you and your employer pay will depend on your earnings and the class you are insured under. Refer to *welfare.ie* for the current rates.

PRSI Refunds

If the wrong rate of PRSI is deducted from your wages you are entitled to a refund. To get a refund either you or your employer should contact the Refunds Section in the Department of Social Protection and you will be sent a refund application form to fill out.

PRSI Refunds Section
Gandon House,
Amiens Street,
Dublin 1
Telephone (01) 673 2586

Employing Family Members and PRSI

Most employees are liable to pay PRSI, but there are exceptions to this rule in the case of certain family employment. This term is used to describe a situation in which a self-employed sole trader either employs, or is assisted in the running of the business by a specified family member(s). However, if the business does not operate on a sole trader basis, for example if it is a limited company or a partnership, it is not considered family employment.

To find out more about the family employment, refer to *welfare.ie* for an information pack.

Social Insurance Payments and Benefits

A wide range of benefits are available to people who have paid social insurance. Your entitlement to these benefits depends on a number of conditions as well as the social insurance contribution requirement. Depending on what payment you are applying for, the social insurance qualifying criteria varies. In general, when you apply for a social insurance payment the following will be examined:

- What class or classes of social insurance you have paid.
- Your age when you started making social insurance contributions (this applies in the case of State pensions).
- The number of paid and/or credited contributions you have made since entering insurable employment
- The number of contributions paid and/or credited in the relevant tax year before the benefit year in which you make the claim.
- The relevant tax year is the second last complete tax year before you make a claim.
- The yearly average number of contributions in the case of some pensions.

The social insurance payments available include:

- Jobseeker's Benefit
- Illness Benefit
- Maternity Benefit
- Adoptive Benefit
- Health and Safety Benefit
- Invalidity Pension
- Widow's, Widower's or Surviving Civil Partner's (Contributory) Pension
- Guardian's Payment (Contributory)
- State Pension (Contributory)
- Treatment Benefit
- Occupational Injuries Benefit
- Carer's Benefit

Maintaining Your Social Insurance

If you leave the workforce, it is important that you keep your social insurance record active. To protect your social insurance record and keep it active, you should contact the Department of Social Protection *welfare.ie* to check if you can get credited contributions. It may be possible in certain circumstances for you to make voluntary contributions.

Ireland also has social security arrangements with other countries that allow you to combine social insurance contributions that you have paid in Ireland with social insurance contributions that you have paid in another country. This can help you to qualify for a social insurance payment in Ireland or in a country with whom Ireland has a social security arrangement.

All records of your insurance contributions are kept and managed by the PRSI Records section in the Department of Social Protection. The Department is responsible for the payments made as a result of your social insurance contributions. You can request a copy of your social insurance record online. To check your social insurance record, you will need your Personal Public Service Number (PPSN). This number is a unique identification number which you need when dealing with state agencies.

9 EDUCATION

Irish Schooling

All children living in Ireland have the right to education, this includes refugees, asylum seekers, or children of migrant workers. They are also entitled to free pre-school, primary, and secondary education, but you will still need to pay for the uniform, books, stationary and for any school trips. There are also private schools where you will need to pay fees every year. School uniforms are quite common in all levels of school, but vary from school to school. There are subsidies available to assist with this.

Although it is most common for children to commence primary school at aged four or five, education is compulsory for all children in Ireland from the ages of six to 16 or until students have completed three years of second level education including one sitting of the Junior Certificate examination.

In the English-speaking regions of Ireland, English is the primary medium of instruction at all levels. The exception to this is the specialised Irish speaking schools, Gaelscoileanna, where Irish is the working language. A student attending a school that receives public money must be taught the Irish language. However, certain students may get an exemption from learning Irish, e.g. students with a learning difficulty or those who have spent a significant period of time overseas.

In the Irish-speaking regions of Ireland, Irish is the primary medium of instruction at all levels. In these schools, English is taught as a second language in the second or third year.

Ireland offers a range of school types from private to public, co-educational to single sex, but some areas may have more limited options. The types of schools available for each level of schooling is discussed further in the following sections. Be aware that although controversial, religious schools, particularly of the Catholic and Protestant denominations, are allowed to give precedence to baptised children in circumstances where demand for places in the school exceeds the number available.

Tips

- To find schools in the area that you are moving to, go onto the Department of Education's website *education.ie* 'Find a School' function.
- You can save money by buying, selling or exchanging second hand school books from the *schooldays.ie* website.

Childcare and Pre-Schooling

Irish Pre-School

Irish Early Childhood Care and Education Scheme (ECCE)

Pre-school is optional in Ireland. Under the ECCE scheme children are entitled to a year of free pre-schooling in the year prior to starting primary schools. Prior to this, parents must pay for their children to attend.

The scheme provides three hours per day, five days per week over 38 weeks and children must be aged between three years two months and four years seven months on 1st September of the year that they commence. If your child attends the care service for longer than this, then you will be charged for that extra time.

Pre-school in Ireland takes the form of privately run crèches, play-schools and Montessori schools. Children can attend for one year or two years at the ages of three and/or four.

Irish Childcare

Full Day Care

Full day care provides children three months to six years structured care for over 3.5 hours a day. Some services may also include after-school care. Providers include day nurseries and crèches.

Sessional Pre-School Service

A sessional pre-school service offers a planned program to pre-school children for up to 3.5 hours per session and generally care for children between the ages of two and six years old. In order to provide the service, a recognised childcare qualification is required.

Options:

- *Montessori groups:* Focus on individualised education where children can independently choose their own activities. Care provided for children up to six years of age.
- *Parent and toddler groups:* A group of parents, guardians or carers who come together with their children for supervised play and companionship.
- *Naíonraí:* Irish speaking nursery schools or play schools.
- *Early Start Program:* A one-year preventative intervention scheme offered in selected schools in designated disadvantaged areas to children aged three and four years old.

Childminders

A childminder cares for children in their own home, sometimes alongside their own children, for more than two hours a day. In some countries this may be called Home or Family Day Care. A childminder can care for up to five children under the age of six years. Parents and childminders arrange their own terms and conditions.

School Age Childcare

Services for schoolchildren can include breakfast clubs, after school clubs and school holiday programs such as summer camps. The service may also include homework supervision, planned activities and a meal.

Au Pair

An au pair is not a professional nanny or childminder. They are typically a young person who lives as part of a host family. They are usually given room and board and paid a weekly allowance of between €80 and €120 in exchange for about 20 hours of services, such as, light housework and/or child minding. This arrangement gives the au pair the opportunity to experience a different culture and improve their foreign language skills.

Irish Childcare Rates

The Irish childcare rates are dependent on the type of childcare you choose, the number of hours and the level of staff training in that facility.

The pre-school education year provided under the Early Childhood Care and Education scheme is free.

For Further Information

The Child and Family Agency website *tusla.ie* is able to provide you essential information such as:

- Tips on choosing a pre-school.
- Inspection Reports on childcare services.
- List of childcare services by county.
- Standard operating services.
- Advice if you have a difficulty or a complaint about a service.

Primary Schooling (Bunscoil)

Children are typically enrolled in the Junior Infant class at the age of either four or five depending on the wishes of their parents and the policy of the school. Some schools require the child be four years of age before a specific date in order to enrol. Otherwise, the child must seek a place in a different school or wait until the next year to enrol.

The National Council for Curriculum and Assessment prepare the Primary School Curriculum which is taught in all schools. It is left to church authorities to formulate and implement the religious curriculum in the schools they control.

Irish Primary School Levels

- Junior Infants *Naíonáin Shóisearacha* – Age 4-5/5-6
- Senior Infants *Naíonáin Shinsearacha* – Age 5-6/6-7
- First Class *Rang a hAon* – Age 6-7/7-8
- Second Class *Rang a Dó* – Age 7-8/8-9
- Third Class *Rang a Trí* – Age 8-9/9-10
- Fourth Class *Rang a Ceathar* – Age 9-10/10-11
- Fifth Class *Rang a Cúig* – Age 10-11/11-12
- Sixth Class *Rang a Sé* – Age 11-12/12-13

Types of Irish Primary Schools

National Schools

Typically controlled by a board of management under diocesan patronage and often include a local clergyman.

Gaelscoileanna Schools

Irish is the language spoken in these schools, but they differ from Irish-language National Schools in Irish-speaking regions in that most are under the patronage of a voluntary organisation, Foras Pátrúnachta na Scoileanna Lán-Ghaeilge, rather than a diocesan patronage.

Multi Denominational Schools

Generally under the patronage of a non-profit limited company without share capital. Many are under the patronage of a voluntary organisation, Educate Together. These schools welcome students from all religions and backgrounds.

Preparatory Schools

Independent, fee-paying primary schools that do not rely on the state for funding. Most are under the patronage of a religious order.

Irish Primary School Hours

Primary school hours are typically 9am to 3pm and the younger children in the Junior and Senior Infant levels usually finish at 2pm. There is a one hour lunch break and most schools allow children to return home to eat as they don't typically provide a cooked meal. Be aware that individual schools may vary.

How to Enrol in Irish Primary Schools

To find schools in your area, go onto the Department of Education's website *education.ie* 'Find a School' function. To apply for a place in an Irish primary school, contact the school directly. It's best to contact the school as soon as possible as most schools have waiting lists in place. Be aware that your child may be required to sit an entrance exam.

Tips

- You can save money by buying, selling or exchanging second hand school books from the *schooldays.ie* website.

Secondary Schooling (Meánscoil)

The Department of Education and Skills develop the Rules and Program for Secondary Schools which sets out the minimum standards of education required at this level. Examinations are overseen by the State Examinations Commission.

Irish Secondary School Levels

Junior Cycle (Timthriall Sóisearach)
- First Year *An Chéad Bhliain* – Age 12–14
- Second Year *An Dara Bliain* – Age 13–15
- Third Year *An Tríú Bliain* – Age 14–16

The Junior Cycle ends with the Junior Certificate Examination. This exam is held in early June. Many schools hold Pre-Certificate Examinations to prepare students around February. These pre-examinations are provided by independent companies and are not mandatory across all schools.

Transition Year (Idirbhliain)

- Transition Year *Idirbhliain* – Age 15–17

The Transition Year is optional in some schools, compulsory in others, and some may not provide it at all. The content of this year is left to the school. The range of activities in the Transition Year varies from school to school, but many include work experience, project work, international trips or exchanges and excursions, and courses such as creative writing, sailing, film-making and public speaking.

The purported benefits of the program are that it allows students to mature and explore career options to assist them when choosing subjects for their senior cycle. However, opponents believe that a year away from traditional study and the classroom environment can cause problems when they return to do the Senior Cycle. The activities can also be very costly and some believe that the activities undertaken in the Transition Year can prevent students from enrolling in the Senior Cycle.

Senior Cycle (Timthriall Sinsearach)

- Fifth Year *An Cúigiú Bliain* – Age 16–18 or if transition year is skipped age 15–17.
- Sixth Year *An Séú Bliain* – Age 17–19 or if transition year is skipped age 16–18.
- The Senior Cycle ends with the Leaving Certificate Examination. This exam is held on the first Wednesday after the June bank holiday. Many schools hold Pre-Certificate Examinations to prepare students around February. These pre-examinations are provided by independent companies and are not mandatory across all schools.

Types of Irish Secondary Schools

Secondary Schools

Owned and managed by religious communities or private organisations. The state funds 90% of teachers' salaries and 95% of other costs.

Vocational Schools

Owned and managed by Education and Training Boards. The state funds 93% of their costs.

Comprehensive Schools or Community Schools

Fully funded by the state, and run by local boards of management.

Gaelcholáistes

Irish is the language spoken in these schools, but they differ from Irish language National Schools in Irish speaking regions in that most are under the patronage of a voluntary organisation, Foras Pátrúnachta na Scoileanna Lán-Ghaeilge, rather than a diocesan patronage.

Grind Schools

Fee paying privately run schools outside the state sector that tend to run only Senior Cycle 5th and 6th year as well as a one year repeat Leaving Certificate program. Some students opt for grinds to improve their grades.

Irish Secondary School Hours

Secondary school hours are typically 9am to 4pm with a one hour lunch break. Most schools allow children to return home to eat as they don't typically provide a cooked meal. Be aware that individual schools may vary.

How To Enrol in Irish Secondary Schools

To apply for a place in an Irish secondary school, contact the school directly. To find schools in your area, go onto the

Department of Education's website *education.ie*. Its best to contact the school as soon as possible as most schools have waiting lists in place. Your child may be required to sit an entrance exam.

Tips

- You can save money by buying, selling or exchanging second hand school books from the *schooldays.ie* website.
- Full time students are eligible to obtain a Student Leap Card which can give you up to 50% discount on Irish Transport as well as nationwide retail discounts.

Higher Education

The Irish higher education system offers a wide range of internationally recognised courses and, as a result, attracts a number of students from abroad. Ireland has five universities and colleges that rank in the top 400 of the Times Higher Education World University Rankings for 2014-2015 (four of them rank in the top 300).

Fees

Irish, EU/EEA and Swiss Students

Under the Free Fees Initiative University Education in Ireland is free, but only for students applying from the European Union who:

- Has EU nationality, or is a national of a member country of the European Economic Area or Switzerland, or has been granted official refugee status.
- Has been a resident in an EU Member State for at least three of the five years preceding entry to the course.
- Must not be undertaking a second undergraduate course.

Although there are no tuition fees for Irish and EU students, there are still the student service fees that need to be paid on registration in order to cover the cost of examinations, insurance, and registration.

Students from Other Countries

If you don't qualify for the Free Fees Initiative, then studying in Ireland is still an attractive option because it offers reasonably priced higher education. Consequently, Ireland attracts a number of international students, particularly Americans, who are enticed by lower fees (compared to their own country) and the exciting experience of living abroad.

Scholarships

For a list of the scholarships available for international students, see the Education in Ireland website *educationinireland.com.*

English Language Requirements

As courses are taught in English, you must be proficient in English in order to be accepted. However, there are many private English language training schools nationwide which offer both short and long-term courses. Some of the universities and colleges also provide English language training courses for those aiming to study with them.

Undergraduate Study in Ireland

Irish and EU Students need to apply to enter an Irish Higher Education Institution (HEI) through the Central Applications Office (CAO) *cao.ie*, rather than the individual institution.

For Irish students, the CAO provides a handbook to students via schools in September which provides information on courses, fees, deadlines etc... EU students can access this CAO handbook online.

You must submit your application to study either online through the CAO website or by post.

For non-EU students, you will need to contact the International Office of the institution that you wish to attend.

Entry Requirements

The entry requirements vary from year to year, depending on the number of places available and the number of applicants. Entry into the more popular courses can be competitive.

Irish students compete for entry based on results achieved in their Leaving Certificate Examination. Students are graded on their six best subject scores.

The International Bacculaureate (IB) Diploma is also accepted as meeting the minimum entry requirement for higher education programs, as all applications are assessed individually. But the Diploma does not guarantee admission and some institutions may stipulate additional requirements.

Medicine

If you want to apply to study medicine in Ireland, you will need to undertake the Health Professions Admissions Test (HPAT). You can access more information about the HPAT at *hpat-ireland.acer.edu.au*. The score achieved in this examination will be added to your Leaving Certificate points to create a total point's score. Students must achieve minimum points, which can change year to year, and also meet the matriculation requirements of the Medical School applied to.

Non-EU applicants will need to contact the International Office of the institution they wish to attend.

Mature Students

Universities also have systems in place for accepting mature students, and students who have successfully completed a Post Leaving Certificate or Further Education courses.

Postgraduate Study in Ireland

Irish, EU and non-EU postgraduate students can apply directly to their preferred institute. However, some colleges may redirect you to apply through the Postgraduate Applications Centre (PAC). The PAC website *pac.ie* provides detailed information about the colleges and courses that are available and also enables you to lodge your application.

Entry-Requirements

Graduate Medical School

If you want to apply for entry to the graduate entry programs you will need to sit the Graduate Medical School Admissions Test (GAMSAT). This exam was developed by the Australian Council for Educational Research (ACER) to assist with the selection of students for graduate medical programs. You can learn more at their website *gamsat.acer.edu.au*.

PhD

phdireland.ie provides an up to date portal of the PhD projects that are available to international students and researchers across a large range of disciplines.

Tips

- Full time students are eligible to obtain a Student Leap Card which can give you up to 50% discount on Irish Transport as well as nationwide retail discounts.

School Holidays

Irish Primary and Secondary School Holidays

Irish School Year

The school year typically commences in September and ends in June.
- The dates for the start and the end of the school year are not standardised.
- The schools set the exact dates for when students finish school in summer and when they start school in autumn. They are generally closed in July and August for the summer holidays.

Irish School Holidays

The dates for the school terms, mid term breaks, Christmas, and Easter are standardised.

Every school must be open for a minimum of:
- 183 days at primary level.
- 167 days at post-primary level.

Schools can use any remaining days at their discretion to extend the summer holiday period or to close on religious or other holidays. However, schools cannot use these days to extend the Christmas, Easter or mid-term breaks (unless a religious observance day/s falls at that time for schools of a particular denomination or faith). If a school does not have enough discretionary days left for a religious holiday, schools can denote that day a non-tuition day.

Holidays vary depending on the school. At the start of the school year, each school will give a list of days that it will be closed during the year, including holidays and training days for teachers.

Generally primary and secondary get similar holidays:

- *Mid-term break:* 1 week off around Halloween.
- *Christmas:* 2 weeks off, generally the last week in December and the first week in January.
- *Mid-term break:* 1 week off in February.
- *Easter:* 2 weeks off.
- *Summer holidays:* Primary schools usually give students July and August off. Secondary schools give students June, July and August off. The exam years, 3rd and 6th year, have about two weeks of exams in June.

Irish Higher Education Holidays

- First semester generally runs from mid to late September, and sometimes early October to December.
- Second semester usually runs from January to mid or late May with a break for Easter of up to a month.

10 TRANSPORT

Public Transport Options

Irelands National Transport Authority

The National Transport Authorities website *transportforireland.ie* is an essential resource for planning your trip anywhere around Ireland. The planner provides timetable and map information from all licensed public transport providers across all of Ireland. It provides plans for trains, buses, trams, ferry, and taxi services and combines them into easy to read journey plans. It provides door-to-door route plans and has information about scheduled departures and trips near your current location and from any specified point. Your plans also can be for now or any time in the future.

Irelands Free Journey Planner App

You can also download the free Journey Planner app from the Apple App Store, Google Play Store or Windows Store.

Journey Planner App Features

- All Ireland coverage including rural locations and cities such as Dublin, Belfast, Cork, Galway, Limerick & Waterford.

- All modes of public transport including trains, buses, and trams from transport providers such as Dublin Bus, LUAS, Bus Eireann, DART, Commuter Rail, AirCoach, GoBe, Matthews Coaches etc...
- Commuter Rail, Air Coach, GoBe, Matthews Coaches etc…
- Dynamic zoom and scroll mapping.
- GPS.
- Saves favourite locations and recent journeys.

Leap Card

The leap card is a pay as you go smart card used on the following public transport:
- Dublin Bus.
- DART and Commuter Rail in Dublin's 'Short Hop Zone'.
- Dublin LUAS.
- Bus Éireann services services in Dublin and surrounding counties (excluding Expressway).
- Bus Éireann services in Cork city, Limerick city, and Galway city.
- City Direct in Galway city.
- Wexford Bus, Swords Express, Collins Coaches and Matthews Coaches services.

There are a range of Leap Cards to choose from and it is much cheaper to use the Leap Card than purchasing paper tickets for each trip. The Leap Cards are the same size as a credit card, so fits easily into your wallet.

Leap Visitor Card: Suitable for short stay visitors in Dublin

The Leap Visitor Card is prepaid ticket that provides you unlimited travel for up to 1, 3 or 7 days on Dublin public transport. This includes:
- The Dublin 747 Airport bus.
- Dublin public buses.
- DART – Dublin's local train service.
- LUAS - Dublin's city tram services.

Where Can I Purchase the Leap Visitor Card?

Purchase your Leap Visitor Card at the arrivals hall at Dublin airport. Go to the Bus and Travel Information Desk in Terminal 1, Spar shop in Terminal 2, or the Discover Ireland Tourist Information Desk in Terminal 2. If you don't arrive via Dublin airport, you can still purchase a Leap Visitor Card in Dublin city centre. Visit Dublin Bus, 59 Upper O'Connell St; Discover Ireland Centre, 14 Upper O'Connell St.; Visit Dublin Centre, 25 Suffolk St.

How Do I Use My Visitor Leap Card?

On the Bus

On the Dublin Bus and Airlink 747, touch the ticket against the Leap Card validator device on the right-hand side as you enter the bus.

On the Train

To get to your train, you will need to touch your card on the Leap Card validator device at the platform entry to get through the electronic gates. Once you get off at your stop touch your card on the Leap Card device to get through the exit gates.

On the LUAS Tram

For the LUAS tram, touch your card on the Leap Card device located on the platform before getting into the tram. When you get off the tram, you need to touch the card on the Leap Card device at the station you are departing from.

Adult Leap Card: Suitable for those living in Ireland or holidaying in Ireland.

The Leap Card is a pay as you go, or 'prepaid' smart card, that can be used on public transport in Dublin, Galway and Cork. The fare is cheaper when using the Leap Card versus paying cash for single tickets.

How Can I Get an Adult Leap Card?

There are three ways you can obtain a Leap Card:

- Online using the *leapcard.ie* website.
- Using a DART or commuter rail ticket machine.
- At one of the Leap Card Agent shops that are identifiable by a pink 'Payzone' logo (find an agent at *payzone.ie*).

Adult Leap Card Ticket Types

You can load a range of tickets onto your Leap Card. You have a number of options depending on which transport operator you use:

Ashbourne Connect: Adult and child weekly tickets.

Bus Éireann: Zonal tickets depending on region.

Collins Coaches: Adult and student 10 trip tickets.

Dublin Bus: 1 day family rambler, 5 day rambler (adult and student), 30 day rambler (adult and student).

Matthews: Adult, Child and Student 10 trip tickets Swords Express: Adult and student 10 trip tickets.

Wexford Bus: Adult, Student and Child 10 journey Weekly tickets. Adult and Student Flexi 10 journey ticket.

Taxsaver Tickets: Employees and directors can receive Annual and Monthly commuter tickets Tax and PRSI (social insurance) free as part of their salary package.

These Taxsaver tickets include monthly and annual tickets from Bus Éireann, Dublin Bus, Irish Rail and Luas. These tickets are ordered through your employer.

For information on the Bus Éireann, Dublin Bus and Irish Rail TaxSaver ticket options, visit *taxsaver.ie*.

For information on the Luas TaxSaver ticket options visit *luas.ie*.

How Much Does the Adult Leap Card Cost?

Leap Cards are free, but to obtain one you must place a minimum of €5 travel credit on it.

How Do I Top-Up My Adult Leap Card?

You can top-up your card online, at any of the Payzone agents, or using the commuter rail ticket machines. Minimum top up is €5.

Student Leap Card: Suitable for full time students

The Student Leap Card provides full time students living in Ireland (including international students) up to 50% discount on Irish Transport as well as nationwide retail discounts.

How Much Does the Student Leap Card Cost?

From 1st September 2016, the Card is €7 by post, or €10 at Student Leap Card Agents (€7, plus a €3 photo capture fee).

How Can I Get the Student Leap Card?

Find a designated Student Leap Card agents near you on their website *studentleapcard.ie*, or download the application form to apply by post.

How Do I Top-Up My Student Leap Card?

You can top-up your card online, at any of the Payzone agents, or using the commuter rail ticket machines. Minimum top up is €5.

Child Leap Card: Suitable for children between 4 and 18 years of age

Children 3 years of age and under can travel on public transport in Ireland for free. Children over 4 years of age can benefit from discounted fares. There are also cheap 'school hours' fares.

There are two types of child Leap Cards:

- 4 to 15 years of age
- 16 to 18 years of age. This card must be personalised, see below.

How Can I Get a Child Leap Card?

There are three ways you can obtain an age 4 to 15 years of age Leap Card:

- Online using the *leapcard.ie* website.
- Using a DART or commuter rail ticket machine.
- At one of the Leap Card Agent shops that are identifiable by a pink 'Payzone' logo (find an agent at *payzone.ie*).

The age 16 to 18 years Leap Card can only be purchased using the Leap Card website *leapcard.ie*. Once your order is submitted, you will receive a reference number via email. Bring this reference number along with your ID (Passport/ Driving Licence/Garda Age Card) to a validation centre so your age can be validated. Then, your card will be sent to you by post, usually within 5 working days.

How Much Does the Child Leap Card Cost?

Leap Cards are free, but to obtain one you must place a minimum of €3 travel credit on it.

How Do I Top-Up My Child's Leap Card?

You can top-up your card online, at any of the Payzone agents, or using the commuter rail ticket machines. Minimum top up is €5.

How Do I Use the Leap Card?

On the Bus

For bus services, touch the card onto the device beside the driver and tell them where you wish to go. They will deduct the correct fare. You do not have to touch off.

On the Train

To get to your train, you will need to touch your card on the Leap Card device at the platform entry to get through the electronic gates. It will deduct the maximum fare. However, once you get off at your stop and touch your card on the Leap Card device to get through the exit gates it will charge the correct fare for your trip and credit your account for the difference. Unless of course your trip cost the maximum amount.

On the LUAS Tram

For the LUAS tram, touch your card on the Leap Card device on the platform before getting into the tram. It will deduct the maximum fare, but when you get off the tram, you need to touch your card to the Leap Card device at the station you are departing at. It will then adjust the fare accordingly and charge you the correct fare for your trip, unless of course your trip cost the maximum amount.

Irish Licensed Private Bus Services

As well as the public bus services, there are also a large number of licensed private bus services operating both city and intercity services throughout Ireland.

Some of the big operators are listed below though the list is not exhaustive:

- **Air Coach** *aircoach.ie*: Provides Dublin airport transfers and transport between Dublin and Cork as well as Dublin and Belfast.
- **Bus Éireann** *buseireann.ie*: Provides transport services throughout Ireland. If you are planning to travel around Ireland using their buses, they also offer an "Open-Road" pass which is valid for travel on Bus Éireann's scheduled services in the Republic of Ireland including Expressway, commuter, local city and town services. For each Open-Road ticket purchased you can avail of 3 days of unlimited travel out of 6 consecutive days. You can extend your trip by purchasing extra "stamps" for your Open-Road ticket.
- **J. J. Kavanagh & Sons** *jjkavanagh.ie:* Transport services between Limerick, Waterford and Clonmel to Shannon and Dublin airport.
- **Finnegan Bray** *finnegan-bray.ie:* Services that link the Southern Cross with Bray Dart and Sandyford LUAS and a night bus from Dublin to Bray, Greystones, Charlesland, and Kilcoole.

- **City Link** *citylink.ie:* Services Ireland's major cities and towns.
- **GoBé** *gobe.ie:* Provides transport services between Dublin and Cork.
- **Go Bus** *gobus.ie:* Provides transport services between Dublin and Galway.

Irish Rail

Iarnród Éireann – Irish Rail, provides train links between Irelands main cities and towns. To book a rail journey and to find out more go to the Irish Rail website *irishrail.ie*.

The Eurail Ireland Pass

Visitors to Ireland can get unlimited travel on the national rail network of the Republic of Ireland and Northern Ireland. You can choose from 3, 4, 5 or 8 days of unlimited travel within a 1 month period and travel days may be used consecutively or non-consecutively. Only non-European residents can travel with a Eurail pass. If you're a European resident you can travel with an Interrail pass.

Before purchasing this pass, just make sure that you are going to get your money's worth by checking the fares to all the places that you plan to visit. Also, be aware that many of the Irish rural areas can only be accessed by bus. To purchase the Eurail Ireland Pass and to learn more, visit *eurail.com*.

Irelands Rail App

You can also download the free Iarnrod Eireann Irish Rail app from the Apple App Store or Google Play Store. The planner provides real time train information including delays and remaining time to departure.

Iarnrod Eireann Irish Rail App Features
- Journey planner (timetables) functionality.
- Augmented Reality – station location services.
- Identification of nearby stations based on current location.

- Details of intermediate stations and whether there are any changes on route.
- Compact display of route alternatives, including door-to-door navigation and walking distances.
- Favourite function for destinations and routes including auto-history for past queries.
- Re-entry on last screen when leaving or re-starting the application.

Irelands Free Travel Scheme

If you are aged 66 years or over and receive a social welfare pension, you are eligible for free travel on Irish public transport. You need not apply as you should be issued the Free Travel Pass automatically. Those under 66 years of age and receiving an Invalidity Pension, Blind Pension, Disability Allowance or Carer's Allowance will also be issued with the pass.

The Government has now introduced a Public Services Card which will eventually replace the Free Travel Pass. If you are entitled to free travel, when you are issued with your new Public Services Card it will also be your Free Travel Card. The card will have F-T printed in a yellow octagon in the top-left-hand corner of the card. You can see a sample card on *welfare.ie*.

You must show your Public Services Card when you are travelling on public transport. In some cases you may be asked to scan your Public Services Card however not all transport operators have this facility. When you receive your new Public Services Card, you must return your old free travel pass to the Department of Social Protection.

There are 3 categories of free travel:
- If FT-P is written on your Public Services Card, you are entitled to free travel.
- If FT+S is written on your Public Services Card, your spouse, partner or cohabitant can join you for free when you are travelling (they cannot travel for free alone). Your spouse, partner or cohabitant's name will not be on the card.

- If FT+C is written on your Public Services Card a companion (over 16) can travel with you for free (because you are unable to travel alone for medical reasons).

Tips

- Learn more about Ireland's Free Travel Scheme at the Citizen Information website *citizensinformation.ie*.

Senior SmartPass for travelling in Northern Ireland

The All Ireland Free Travel Scheme allows a Free Travel cardholder to travel free of charge on all bus and rail services within Northern Ireland using a Senior Smartpass card. Similarly, Northern Ireland Senior Smartpass holders are entitled to travel for free on services in Ireland using their existing Senior Smartpass.

If you wish to access the All Ireland Free Travel scheme within Northern Ireland you will need to first get a Senior SmartPass card by filling in an application form FTNI1. Unfortunately you can't get this form online, to get one you will need to contact your social welfare local office.

The application form must be returned in person (not posted) to your social welfare local office, and you must bring the following items with you to your social welfare local office:

Your current Free Travel Pass/Public Services Card

Evidence of your address, (for example, a gas, electricity, phone bill or bank statement)

Evidence of your identity, (for example, your drivers licence, passport or another form of photo identification)

A recent passport standard colour photograph.

It may take up to six weeks to process your application. However you can only apply 3 weeks before your 66th birthday. If you apply more than 3 weeks before your 66th birthday, your application will be rejected.

Your Senior SmartPass will expire after 5 years.

Local Public Transport

Dublin Public Transport

Leap Card

The Leap Card can be used on all Dublin public transport. Visitors to Dublin should consider purchasing the Leap Visitor Card which is a prepaid ticket that provides you unlimited travel for up to 72 hours/3 days on Dublin public transport.

Dublin Tram Network

Dublin city has a tram network called the LUAS *luas.ie* which consists of two line:

- *Red Line:* 20kms in length and 32 Stops, the Red Line runs from Tallaght to The Point and from Saggart to Connolly.
- *Green Line:* 16.5km in length and 22 Stops, the Green Line runs from Brides Glen to St. Stephen's Green through Sandyford.

There are electronic displays at each stop advising you of when the next tram is due, as well as announcements. The Dublin Transport Real Time Ireland App can be used in conjunction with this service. The trams tend to get very cramped, so be prepared to squeeze yourself in.

Dublin LUAS Tram Ticketing

You can purchase your tram ticket from the ticket machine located at each stop, but for a cheaper fare use a Leap Card.

How Do I Use My Leap Card on the LUAS Tram?

Touch your card on the Leap Card device on the platform before getting into the tram. It will deduct the maximum fare, but when you get off the tram, you need to touch your card to the Leap Card device at the station you are departing at. It will then adjust the fare accordingly and charge you the correct fare for your trip, unless of course your trip cost the maximum amount.

Dublin Buses

Dublin City Buses

Buses are the most widely used form of public transport in Dublin city. They are operated by Dublin Bus *dublinbus.ie*. The

Bus Arrival Information Service is based on the GPS locations of buses, provides real time estimates of bus arrivals on electronic information boards at each stop. The Dublin Transport Real Time Ireland App can be used in conjunction with this service.

Dublin Commuter Buses

- **Matthews Coaches** *matthews.ie*: Between Dublin, Dundalk and Bettystown.
- **Swords Express** *swordsexpress.com*: Between Dublin and Swords.
- **Wexford Bus** *wexfordbus.ie*: Between Dublin and Wexford.
- **Collins Coaches** *collinscoaches.ie*: Between Dublin and Carrickmacross and once a day to Ballybay.

Dublin Bus Ticketing

You can purchase your ticket from the driver on board the bus, but for a cheaper fare use a Leap Card.

How Do I Use My Leap Card on the Bus?

Touch your Leap Card onto the device located beside the driver and tell them where you wish to go. They will deduct the correct fare. You do not need to touch off.

On the Airlink 747 bus, touch the ticket against the Leap Card validator device on the right-hand side as you enter the bus. However, if you want a cheaper return ticket, you will need to purchase it with cash from the driver. Make sure you keep the ticket in a safe place as you will need it for your return trip.

Dublin Commuter Rail System

Dublin has a commuter rail system. There are four main lines, designated Northern Commuter, Western Commuter, South Eastern Commuter, and South Western Commuter. The trains are operated by Irish Rail *irishrail.ie*.

The Dublin Area Rapid Transit (locally known as the DART) serves the Dublin bay commuter belt:

- Northern Commuter – Dublin Pearse to Dundalk.
- South Eastern Commuter – Dublin Connolly to Wicklow.

- South Western Commuter – Dublin Heuston to Kildare.
- Western Commuter – Dublin Pearse / Docklands to Longford.
- Dublin Area Rapid Transit (DART) – Greystones to Howth / Malahide.

There are electronic displays at each stop advising you of when the next train is due, as well as announcements. The Dublin Transport Real Time Ireland App can be used in conjunction with this service.

Dublin DART Ticketing

You can purchase your train ticket from the ticket machine located at each stop, but for a cheaper fare use a Leap Card.

How Do I Use My Leap Card on the Train?

To get to your train, you will need to touch your card on the Leap Card device at the platform entry to get through the electronic gates. It will deduct the maximum fare. However, once you get off at your stop and touch your card on the Leap Card device to get through the exit gates. It will charge the correct fare for your trip and credit your account for the difference, unless of course your trip cost the maximum amount.

Dublin Transport Real Time Ireland App

You can download the free Real Time Ireland app from the Apple App Store or the Google Play Store. It provides real time data for Dublin Bus, Bus Éireann, DART, LUAS and Irish Rail. It also gives reminders to notify you when the bus is approaching your stop, or when you are near a certain bus stop, enables you to create reminders and access travel updates etc…

Real Time Ireland App Features

- Allows you to set alerts to inform you when your bus is 10, 20 or 30 minutes away from a certain bus stop, so you can plan when to leave home or work.
- Informs you when you are approaching a particular bus stop.

- View Stops and Routes on a map and navigate through the map for additional stops and information.
- Transport updates from Dublin Bus, Bus Éireann, LUAS, DART and Iarnród Éireann.
- Setup favourites so that you can access the Real Time passenger information for your regular stops quickly.

Cork Public Transport

Leap Card

The Leap Card can be used on the Cork bus services and the Cork – Cobh / Midleton train lines.

Cork Buses

The city buses are run by Bus Éireann *buseireann.ie* which services areas like Cork City, Knocknaheeny, Ballinlough, Cork, Mahon, Cork, Mayfield, Cork, Frankfield, Cork, Ballintemple and Farranree, Cork and suburban routes serving towns such as Glanmire, Ballincollig, Carrigaline, Douglas, Midleton, Mallow, Cobh and Goleen.

Cork Bus Ticketing

You can purchase your ticket from the driver on board the bus, but for a cheaper fare use a Leap Card.

How Do I Use My Leap Card on the Bus?

Touch your Leap Card onto the device located beside the driver and tell them where you wish to go. They will deduct the correct fare. You do not need to touch off.

Cork Trains

There are 3 suburban train lines in the Cork suburban rail service is run by Irish Rail *irishrail.ie*.
- Cork Kent – Blarney ED – Mallow
- Cork Kent – Glanmire – Cobh
- Cork Kent – Glanmire – Midleton

Cork Train Ticketing

You can purchase your train ticket from the ticket machine located at each stop, but for a cheaper fare use a Leap Card.

How Do I Use My Leap Card on the Train?

To get to your train, you will need to touch your card on the Leap Card device at the platform entry to get through the electronic gates. It will deduct the maximum fare. However, once you get off at your stop and touch your card on the Leap Card device to get through the exit gates. It will charge the correct fare for your trip and credit your account for the difference, unless of course your trip cost the maximum amount.

Cork Car Ferry

There is a car river ferry *scottcobh.ie* which runs between Rushbrooke and Passage West.

Cork Ferry Ticketing

No advance purchase / bookings necessary and there are commuter weekly tickets available.

Limerick Public Transport

Leap Card

The Leap Card can be used on the Limerick urban buses run by Bus Éireann.

Limerick Buses

The Limerick urban area is covered mainly by buses run by Bus Éireann *buseireann.ie* and a few routes operated by Euro Bus Limerick *eurobuslimerick.com*. The routes service areas such as Raheen, Dooradoyle, Ballycummin, University of Limerick, O'Malley Park, Caherdavin and Castletroy.

Limerick Bus Ticketing

You can purchase your ticket from the driver on board the bus, but for a cheaper fare use a Leap Card.

How Do I Use My Leap Card on the Bus?

Touch your Leap Card onto the device located beside the driver and tell them where you wish to go. They will deduct the correct fare. You do not have to touch off.

Limerick Trains

The Limerick suburban rail networks are operated by Irish Rail *irishrail.ie* which provides three lines.
- Limerick railway station – Ennis
- Limerick railway station – Nenagh
- Limerick railway station – Tipperary

Limerick Train Ticketing

You can purchase your train ticket from the ticket machine, booth or online. There are a range of ticket types that can be purchased including single, return, off-peak, weekly and monthly tickets.

Galway Public Transport

Leap Card

The Leap Card can be used on Galway bus services.

Galway Buses

Galway Transport *galwaytransport.info* provides information about public transport services currently operating in Galway city and the surrounding area. It includes a summary map of all city bus service routes, a detailed map and timetable link for each route, as well as specific instructions about getting to popular places (work and recreation) using public transport. There are two companies providing bus services throughout the city – Bus Éireann and Galway City Direct. The Leap card can be used on both bus services.

Galway Bus Ticketing

You can purchase your ticket from the driver on board the bus, but for a cheaper fare use a Leap Card.

How Do I Use My Leap Card on the Bus?

Touch your Leap Card onto the device located beside the driver and tell them where you wish to go. They will deduct the correct fare. You do not need to touch off.

Galway Trains

Irish Rail *irishrail.ie* operates Galways Suburban Rail has a rail line connecting Galway and the satellite towns of Oranmore and Athenry. Currently the Leap card cannot be used for the rail services in Galway.

Galway Train Ticketing

You can purchase your train ticket from the ticket machine, booth or online. There are a range of ticket types that can be purchased including single, return, off-peak, weekly and monthly tickets.

Taxi Services

The National Transport Authority is responsible for the licensing and regulation of small service vehicles in Ireland which includes taxis, hackneys, and limousines.

Ireland's vehicle hire services provide wheelchair accessible taxis and hackneys.

What Are Hackneys?

You may hear the term 'hackney' being used. This refers to a private hire vehicle. They fall under the same licensing and regulation laws, but the cabs are pre-booked. They do not have taxi meters so the fare must be pre-agreed between the driver and passenger before the journey begins. Be aware that they cannot be hailed down in a public place.

These days modern hackneys can be booked via an app on your phone. Both Hailo (British) and Uber (American) hackney services are available in Ireland.

Get an Estimate of Your Fare

To give you an idea of what your fare will cost and to help you avoid being ripped off, the Transport of Ireland have a Taxi Fare Estimator tool on the *transportofireland.ie* website.

Check If Your Driver Is Properly Licensed

There are several ways that the National Transport Authority assists you to verify that the vehicle you are about to hire has been correctly registered and the driver has the appropriate licensing to operate the vehicle.

There are two ways to verify:

- Use the Check If a Driver Is Properly Licensed feature on the *transportofireland.ie* website and type in the necessary information.
- You can also download the free Driver Check app from the Apple App Store or for Android devices from the Google Play Store.

This service provides verification for Ireland's licensed taxis, hackneys, limousines and Public Service Vehicles and covers rural locations as well as cities such as Dublin, Cork, Galway, Limerick, and Waterford.

Users can search by the car registration number, the vehicle taxi licence number, the driver licence number or by scanning the appropriate QR codes. There is also the facility to email a friend the trip details.

Customer Information Cards

The *transportofireland.ie* website provides an easy to read guides including the 'Taxi Information Card', 'Hackney Information Card', and 'Limousine Information Card' that gives passengers the necessary information that they need when hiring a service vehicle. These information cards explain what to expect and what to look out for. Taxi's typically carry these information cards and you can usually find them in the pocket behind the drivers seat.

Cycling

City Bike Scheme

- The Dublin scheme was created first and has a different website *dublinbikes.ie*.
- The Cork, Limerick and Galway scheme share the same website *bikeshare.ie*.

Both websites are very easy to navigate and provide all the information you need.

Cycling is becoming an increasingly popular way to get around in Ireland. The Irish cities Dublin, Cork, Limerick and Galway provide public bike schemes. The schemes are continually improving and expanding. Even if you do plan to purchase a vehicle, it's worth considering signing up for the city bikes because they make it so much easier (and cheaper) to get around the city. Cycling enables you to avoid the stress of finding and paying for a car park and dealing with frustratingly slow traffic. The bikes even come with a bike lock, enabling you to pull up and leave your bike to explore on foot.

Short Term Use

The City bikes are available for short term use, which makes them perfect for using while on holiday or if you want to try them out before subscribing to the scheme. The scheme offers a pay as you go service, with the first 30 minutes free, or you can get a cheap 3-day pass.

Not all of the terminals in the Dublin scheme have a credit card facility for short term use payments, so be sure to check the *dublinbikes.ie* website which provides a detailed list of the ones that do.

Annual Pass

Public transport can be rather expensive, but purchasing the annual pass and making use of the city bikes will save you lots of money that you can spend on more exciting things. You also don't have the cost of buying or maintaining the bike, the annoyance of having to store it, or the risk of it being stolen. You will also be improving your health by getting some exercise (which will help offset all those pints of beer you've been drinking).

To subscribe to an annual pass, you need to register online.

Free City Bike Scheme App

Avoid the disappointment of turning up at a bike stand and finding it empty. Download the free app that enables you to find station locations, check bike and stand availability, plan your route and access your account information and activity.

Dublin: To access the free city bike scheme app for Dublin, download the AllBikesNow app from the Apple App Store or the Google Play Store.

Cork, Limerick, and Galway: To access the free city bike scheme app for Cork, Limerick, and Galway, download the *bikeshare.ie* app from the Apple App Store or the Google Play Store.

Tips

- To help you get around, use the Cycle Planner on the Transport of Ireland website *journeyplanner.ie*.

Irelands Cycle Planner

The Transport of Ireland website *journeyplanner.ie* offers a Cycle Planner. Based on your individual cycling capabilities, the Cycle Planner provides information on the best cycling routes in Dublin, Cork, Galway, Limerick, and Waterford.

Irelands Free Cycle Planner App

You can use the Cycle Planner online or download the free Cycle Planner app from the Apple App Store or the Google Play Store. The app provides loads of great features. If you are new to cycling or lack confidence, the Cycle Planner will find a route that avoids roads with heavy traffic and difficult turns at busy junctions to help you gain confidence cycling around town. For the more advanced cyclists, the Cycle Planner will provide the most direct routes to take whilst still recommending cycle tracks where they exist.

There is also a feature called 'Turn Difficulty Factor' that helps you to choose junctions and turns that suit your cycling capability. To save on data roaming, you can save your routes and use them offline.

Cycle Planner App Features

- Find a cycle route via several stop offs.
- Featured themed routes.
- Route options
  - *Easier Routes*: Avoid heavy traffic.
  - *Balanced Routes*: Expect some traffic.
  - *Direct Routes:* Possible heavy traffic.
- Navigation / audible warnings when off route.
- Use the City Bike Hire.
- Avoid hills and difficult junction manoeuvres.
- Elevation information.
- Co2 calculator.
- Calorie counter which also converts them into squares of chocolate!
- Places of interest near your route.
- Take your bike on the train.
- Integrates with the public transport National Journey Planner.
- Save routes for offline use.

Cycle to Work Scheme

The Cycle to Work Scheme is a tax incentive to encourage employees to cycle to work. Under the scheme employers can pay for bicycles and bicycle equipment for their employees and the employee then pays the employer back through a salary sacrifice arrangement of up to 12 months. The employee is not liable for tax, PRSI or the Universal Social Charge on their repayments.

The bicycle and safety equipment must be used for the whole or part (e.g. between home and train station) of a journey between your home and your place of work. Employers do not have to monitor this but you will be asked to sign a statement saying that the bicycle is for your own use and will be mainly used for these journeys.

The scheme applies to new bicycles and pedelecs (electrically assisted bicycles which require some effort from the cyclist) and doesn't cover motorbikes, scooters or mopeds. Generally you select the equipment you want and have the shop invoice your employer directly for the cost. Be aware that the tax exemption does not apply if you pay for the bicycle and are reimbursed by your employer – they must pay for the bicycle. There is a limit of €1,000 on the amount that can be spent and this includes the bicycle, safety equipment and delivery charges. If you spend more than this limit you will be liable for a benefit-in-kind income tax charge.

Purchase of the following new safety equipment is covered in this scheme:

- Cycle helmets which conform to European standard EN 1078
- Bells and bulb horns
- Lights, including dynamo packs
- Mirrors and mudguards to ensure that the rider's visibility is not impaired
- Cycle clips and dress guards
- Panniers, luggage carriers and straps to allow luggage to be safely carried
- Locks and chains to ensure cycle can be safely secured
- Pumps, puncture repair kits, cycle tool kits and tyre sealant to allow for minor repairs
- Reflective clothing along with white front reflectors and spoke reflectors

To access the Cycle to Work Scheme, contact your employer.

11 DRIVING

How to Drive in Ireland

Driving in another country can be stressful, especially if it means driving on the other side of the road and being confronted with new driving challenges such as the dreaded roundabout. But don't despair, with a little bit of preparation you too can gain the necessary knowledge that you need to tackle those Irish roads with confidence.

Road rules

- Drive on the left side of the road.
- Speed is measured in kilometres per hour (km/h). 1km is equal to 0.62miles.
- The speed limits will be clearly displayed on a road sign.
- Generally:
  - Motorways are 120km/h (75 mph).
  - National roads (primary and secondary roads) are 100km/h (62mph).
  - Non-national roads (regional and local) roads are 80km/h (50mph).
  - Roads in built up areas such as towns and cities are 50km/h (31mph).
  - School zones are 30km/h (19mph).

- If you are towing something, then the maximum speed you can go on the motorways and national roads is 80km/h (50mph). There are also speed limits that apply to buses and trucks.
- Yield to emergency vehicles.
- You are required to have the following documents when driving:
  - Vehicle title / registration certificate or vehicle rental agreement.
  - National Car test.
  - Motor Tax.
  - Motor vehicle insurance.
  - An accepted driver's licence.
- At roundabouts, give way to your right.

How to Drive on a Roundabout

For those of you who are unfamiliar with roundabouts, they can be daunting. But follow this information to help you get to more familiar with them.

1. Because all traffic in Ireland drives on the left hand side of the road, the roundabouts go clockwise.
2. When you approach a roundabout slow down and prepare to give way. You have to give way to traffic already on the roundabout but if the road is clear you may proceed.
3. There are many roundabouts in and around City Centres, Main Road Junctions and entrances and exits to Dual Carriageways (Two lanes each way).
4. You will also find roundabouts in and around city centres, main road junctions, entrances and exits to dual carriageways (two lanes each way), on exits from Motorways, and in some built up locations. They are built to effectively replace traffic lights at junctions to allow for a smoother flow of traffic.
5. You may also encounter what we call "mini roundabouts". These are effectively smaller and are basically small raised areas in the centre of a junction. The same rules apply to these as above.
6. If this is your first time to encounter a roundabout, take care. Approach with caution and only proceed when your exit is

clear.

Safety Regulations

- Seatbelts are compulsory for all occupants of the vehicle.
- Children under 12 years of age must not travel in the front seat of the vehicle.
- Babies and children under 3 years, as well as children under 150cm and weighing less then 36kg, must use the correct child seat or booster seat.
- Motorcyclists are required to wear helmets.
- Drink and drug driving is an offence in Ireland. The Garda (police) carry out random drink and drug driving checks. If you refuse, they will take you down to the local Garda office for a blood and urine test. If you continue to refuse testing then you can face disqualification from driving. The legal limit for fully licensed drivers is 50 milligrams of alcohol per 100ml of blood. The legal limit for professional and learner drivers is 20 milligrams of alcohol per 100ml of blood.
- It is illegal to hold a mobile phone while driving.
- If you are involved in an accident, you must stop at the scene.

What to Do in an Accident

If you are involved in an accident, you must stop at the scene, no matter how extensive the damage is. Take the details of the other driver:

- Name
- Address
- Vehicle owner details (it may not be the owner of the vehicle that is driving at the time of the accident).
- Insurance details

If anyone is injured in the accident and/or there is property damage, you should report it to the Garda (police).

If you can, you should also take photographs of the scene of the accident and all damaged property (try to include the entire vehicle in case damage occurs after the accident and they attempt to attribute it to the accident). This can be submitted to the insurance company and Garda if necessary.

Tips

- The emergency number for the Garda and ambulance services is 112 or 999.

What to Expect When Driving Around Ireland

- Because Ireland drives on the left side of the road, they drive right-hand drive vehicles, meaning the driver sits on the right side of the car with the front passenger on the left.
- Most cars in Ireland are manual drive. When hiring a car, you will find that automatics come at a premium.
- Irish roads are generally in good condition with a decent network of highways. However, country roads can be narrow and windy, so take care and drive with caution.
- Road signs are in English and sometimes also Irish.
- In city areas, especially Dublin, expect traffic to be slow at all times throughout the day. You can also expect narrow roads and one way roads.
- Parking is limited in the city areas, particularly Dublin. Don't be tempted to park illegally as they love to clamp and impound cars.
- Look out for delivery vehicles and trucks that pull over in no stopping zones to make their deliveries. Be patient and ready to wait if the road is too narrow to go around them.
- Expect lots of roundabouts.
- Ireland operate speed cameras, however, there are not as many as you may expect in the UK and Australia.
- Like in many European countries, petrol prices in Ireland are particularly high. This is partially due to the steep fuel taxes.
- Irish people tend to drive quite fast, especially the locals who know the road much better than you. Make sure that

you regularly pull over to let people get past you. Although the country roads are narrow, there are usually plenty of areas that you can safely pull over.

- Ireland has toll roads. If you wish to avoid them then most GPS's have this option. However, the alternative route can be much slower.
- Expect walkers, cyclists and farm traffic such as escaped animals grazing on the road side or animals being herded, tractors and machinery as well as horses being ridden or pulling wagons. Horse traffic is even common in the city areas!
- In gloomy, overcast conditions, turn your headlights on to help you be seen by others on the road.
- Take your time and expect it to take longer than you may be used to get to your destination.
- A GPS is a good investment!

Tips

- For further information about the Irish road rules and regulations, visit Ireland's Road Safety Authority website *rulesoftheroad.ie*. Their website allows you to view, download, and listen to the Irish road rules.

Toll Roads

There are eleven toll roads in the Republic of Ireland:
- M50 Barrier-Free Toll
- M1 (Gormanston – Monasterboice)
- M3 (Clonee – Kells)
- M4 (Kilcock – Enfield – Kinnegad)
- M7/M8 (Portlaoise – Castletown / Portlaoise – Cullahill)
- N6 (Galway – Ballinasloe)
- N8 (Rathcormac – Fermoy Bypass)
- N25 (Waterford City Bypass)
- Limerick Tunnel
- East-Link Bridge
- Dublin Port Tunnel

Everyone who drives through these toll roads is expected to pay, regardless of whether you are just visiting Ireland. All of the toll roads, except the M50, have conventional barriers where you can pay cash as you drive through.

The M50 operates a barrier free tolling system. If you intend to travel on the M50 in a rental car, you should contact your car rental company in advance to find out if your rental agreement covers the payment of toll charges. Some companies will include toll charges in your bill; others will require that you pay all toll charges yourself.

If you are required to pay toll charges, you can pay for your M50 journey using any of the following methods:

- Online at *eFlow.ie* – select 'I Want to Pay a Toll' on the home page and follow the page guidelines.
- In person with cash or card at any retail outlet nationwide that has the Payzone sign.
- Phone one of the customer service agents on LoCall: 1890 50 10 50 from the Republic of Ireland, 0845 30 15 405 from the UK, or +800 50 10 50 11 from any other country. If you are having difficulties with these numbers please try +353 1 4610122.

If you live in Ireland and plan to regularly travel through the tolls, then you can set up an account with eFlow and get an electronic tag for your vehicle. This will also give you a cheaper rate for the M50 toll.

If you are only an occasional user of the M50, you can sign up for a Video Account. As you pass through the M50 barrier free tolling system, the cameras will read your registration plate and charge you accordingly. You will also receive a discount on your toll.

Driving Offences Penalty Points System

Ireland has a penalty points system for driving offences. Find out more about the penalty points, fixed charges, and bans on Ireland's Road Safety website *rulesoftheroad.ie*.

Vehicle Breakdown Services

Don't risk being stuck with a broken down vehicle in the middle of the Irish countryside. Get peace of mind by signing up for breakdown cover. If you are hiring a car, this service should be provided by the car hire company.

If you have comprehensive insurance, then breakdown service may be provided as part of your cover. However, the service that they provide may be limited, so check before joining any breakdown service.

The main Irish providers of breakdown services are:
- The AA *theaa.ie*
- Axa *axa.ie*
- Blue Insurance *blueinsurance.ie*
- Breakdown Cover *breakdowncover.ie*
- Car Protect *carprotect.ie*
- Road Rescue *roadrescue.ie*

Traffic Reports

Listen out for traffic reports using:
- The local radio stations.
- AA Roadwatch on their website *theaa.ie*.
- National Roads Authority website *nratraffic.ie*. As well as their website, they also have a free app NRA Traffic from the Google Play Store or the Apple App Store.

Driver Licensing

Renting a Vehicle

When renting a vehicle you will need a full driver's licence from the country that you reside in. However, typically you must have held that licence for 2 years. Drivers aged between 21 – 25 years and 70 – 75 years are usually subject to special conditions.

Non-EU/EEA driving licences cannot be accepted if the holder has been a resident in Ireland for more than 12 months (see below about exchanging your foreign drivers licence).

Typically, an International Driving License is required if your national driver's license is not in Roman script. International Driving Permits must be accompanied by the original domestic licence of the driver. Those that accept non Roman script licences will require an English translation. Always read the fine print of the car hire contract before confirming your booking.

EU/EEA Drivers Licences

If you have an EU/EEA driver's licence you may continue to drive in Ireland on your current licence. You can exchange it for an Irish drivers licence when it expires.

Non EU/EEA Drivers Licences

If you have a licence from a country outside of the EU/EEA, you may drive on your driver's licence in Ireland for 12 months. However, after the 12 month period you need to apply to have your driver's licence changed to an Irish one.

How to Exchange Your Foreign Driving Licence

Are You Eligible to Exchange Your Foreign Driving Licence for an Irish Driving Licence?

To be eligible to exchange your driver's licence for an Irish one you must:

- Permanently reside in Ireland for at least 185 days per year.
- Lived in Ireland for the 12 months prior to applying for the exchange.
- Have an Irish PPS number.
- Have a driver's licence from one of the following countries:
  - Australia (Victorian licence holders must sign a declaration to allow Vic Roads licensing authority to release information to the NDLS if required see *ndls.ie.*)
  - Gibraltar
  - Guernsey
  - Isle of Man
  - Japan

- Jersey
- Manitoba State of Canada (Manitoba licence holders can exchange a Class 5, I of F driving licence for the category B car restricted to automatic transmission, Class 6, stage I and F driving licence for the category A1 small motorcycle. You will also be given a category W Tractor).
- New Zealand (Motorcycle and Car are the only.)
- Ontario State of Canada (Ontario licence holders can exchange a G or G1 driving licence for the category B restricted to automatic transmission.)
- South Africa
- South Korea
- Switzerland
- Taiwan (Motorcycle & Car are the only.)

If you do not have a driver's licence from one of these listed countries, you will need to apply for an Irish drivers licence by completing the full Irish driver licensing procedure.

To exchange your driving licence for an Irish one, you need to make an appointment at the NDLS, which you can do online at *ndls.ie*. If you go into the NDLS centre without an appointment, then expect to wait a while.

What to Bring to Your NDLS Appointment (see the website *ndls.ie* for more information)

- Your driving licence.
- Photographic ID.
- Proof of your residency entitlement.
- Evidence of your PPS Number.
- Proof of address.
- Completed Medical Report Form (if applicable).
- Completed Eyesight Report Form D502 (if applicable).
- A completed Driving licence application Form D401.
- You will also need to pay the appropriate fee.

What to Expect at Your NDLS Appointment

During your NDLS appointment, you will be asked to provide your documentation. They will then take your photograph and capture your signature digitally to print onto your new driver's licence.

Once you have completed the application process and paid for your licence, you will be given a receipt. Your application will be sent to the Central Licensing Processing Unit (CLPU) and your new licence should be posted to you within five to eight working days.

During your NDLS appointment, you will be asked to provide your documentation. They will then take your photograph and capture your signature digitally to print onto your new driver's licence.

Once you have completed the application process and paid for your licence, you will be given a receipt. Your application will be sent to the Central Licensing Processing Unit (CLPU) and your new licence should be posted to you within five to eight working days.

How to Apply for an Irish Driving Licence

If your driver's licence is not from a country listed above, you may drive on your licence for 12 months. But after this period, you must apply for an Irish driving licence by completing the full Irish driver licensing procedure.

In order to apply for an Irish driving licence, you must:
- Be 17 years of age, or, 16 years to drive a work vehicle.
- Demonstrate that you are an Irish Resident.
- Reside in Ireland for at least 185 days per year.
- Have resided in Ireland for 12 months prior to undertaking the driver licence testing process.
- Have an Irish PPS number.

There are five steps that you must complete in order to achieve your full Irish drivers licence:

Step 1: Driver Theory Test (DTT)

There are different tests depending on which category of drivers licence you are applying for. For example, the category B car theory test consists of 40 questions of which 35 must be answered correctly within 45 minutes. Tests are normally done on a computer and can be taken in English or Irish.

To prepare for the test, study the approved DTT Revision material, see the DTT *theorytest.ie*.

How to Book Your DTT

Go online to the DTT website *theorytest.ie* and:
1. Choose the category of licence that you wish to be tested for.
2. Provide the following documents (these documents must be taken with you to your DTT appointment).
    * Valid proof of identity.
    * Evidence of your Irish PPS number.
    * Two identical colour passport sized photos.
3. Select the DTT centre that you wish to attend.
4. Schedule your DTT time.
5. Pay your DTT test fee.

Step 2: Learner Driving Permit

Once you have your theory test certificate, you can apply for a learner driving permit.

How to Make an Appointment at the NDLS

To apply for a learner driving permit, you need to make an appointment at the NDLS, which you can do online. If you go in without an appointment, then expect to be waiting a while.

What to Bring to Your NDLS Appointment
1. Completed Application Form for a Learners Permit D201.
2. Photographic ID.
3. Proof of your entitlement to residency.
4. Evidence of your Irish PPS number.
5. Evidence of your current address.

6. Completed Eyesight Report Form D502.
7. Completed Medical Report Form (if applicable).
8. Current or previous driving licence (if applicable).
9. Driver theory test certificate.
10. You will also need to pay the appropriate Learners Permit fee.

What to Expect at Your NDLS Appointment

During your NDLS appointment, you will be asked to provide your documentation. They will then take your photograph and capture your signature digitally to print onto your new driver's licence.

Once you have completed the application process and paid for your licence, you will be given a receipt. Your application will be sent to the Central Licensing Processing Unit (CLPU) and your new licence should be posted to you within five to eight working days.

Step 3: Essential Driver Training (EDT)

The EDT is a mandatory course that teaches fundamental driving skills. It consists of 12 one-hour lessons. You will also need an experienced driver to supervise your driving practice outside of these lessons. Your lessons and driving practice should be recorded on a specially issued logbook.

The fee for the EDT varies. To find an EDT instructor, visit the RSA website *rsa.ie*.

Important

- Learner drivers must display their "L" plates while they are driving.
- Learner drivers are not allowed to drive on motorways.
- Learner drivers must always be accompanied by a qualified driver (holders of a full driver's licence for at least two years).

Step 4: Driving Test

Once you have completed your EDT and held your learner

driving permit for at least six months, you may book your driving test on the Road Safety Authority website *rsa.ie*. Alternatively you can download a driving test application form or obtain a copy from any motor tax office. The test can be taken in English or Irish. It is recommended that the driving test be applied for well in advance as waiting times can be long.

When taking the driving test, the following are required:

- Pay the necessary driving test fee.
- Your valid learner driving permit.
- Your EDT logbook.
- Evidence of your PPS.
- A roadworthy, registered, insured, motor taxed vehicle.
- L-plates on both the front and rear of the car.

What to Expect During Your Driving Test

There are two components to the test:

1. *Technical check of vehicle:* You must demonstrate how to do a technical check on the car (e.g. check tyres, lights, engine oil etc...)
2. *Practical test:* You will be asked to drive for approximately 30 minutes and to carry out manoeuvres such as, reversing around a corner, parking, hill start etc...

After the driving test has been successfully passed, you will be issued a certificate of competency which is valid for two years. You can use this Certificate of Competency to apply for your full driver's licence.

Step 5: Full Driving Licence

After passing the practical driving test and receiving your Certificate of Competence, you can apply for a full driving licence.

You will need to provide the following documents when applying for a full driving licence:

- A completed application form D401.
- Your learner permit.
- Your Certificate of Competency.
- Completed Medical Report Form (if applicable).

- Evidence of your Irish PPS number.
- Evidence of your address.
- The relevant fee.

Important

- You must display "N" plates while driving for a period of two years after receiving your full Irish drivers licence.
- After passing the practical driving test and receiving your Certificate of Competence, you can apply for a full driving licence.

Owning a Vehicle

Car ownership in Ireland is expensive. There are numerous taxes that must be paid and the cost of petrol is very high. In addition, if you live in a busy city area like Dublin, then parking is limited and expensive. Before purchasing a car, consider whether you really need one. You may be financially better off using public transport, taxi's, city bikes, and the occasional car hire for those times when you want to leave the city (however, there are also very good intercity public transport options).

Value Added Tax (VAT)

You are liable to pay the standard Value Added Tax (VAT) when you purchase a vehicle in Ireland.

You may also be liable to pay VAT for new vehicles that you import into Ireland, even if you paid VAT in the country that you purchased it from. However, if you can provide evidence that the car has been used for at least six months and the vehicle has travelled over 6,000 kilometres when you register it, then you may be able to avoid paying VAT.

Learn more about Irelands VAT rates at *revenue.ie*.

Vehicle Registration Tax (VRT)

Vehicle Registration (VRT) must be paid on all new vehicles purchased in Ireland as well as on vehicles that you import into Ireland.

If you purchase the vehicle from a motor dealer in Ireland, then the dealer is obliged to pay the VRT and register the vehicle before handing it over to you.

If you import a vehicle into Ireland, you will be responsible for registering the vehicle and having it assessed for VRT within seven days of it arriving in Ireland. To do this you will need to take the vehicle to a National Car Testing Service (NCTS) centre *ncts.ie*. At the NCTS they will establish how much VRT you will be required to pay. You can get an estimate of this amount payable from the Revenue Vehicle Registration Online Enquiry System at *ros.ie*.

The registration process must be completed within 30 days of the vehicle arriving in Ireland. Once it has been registered and the VRT paid, you will receive the vehicle registration certificate. This also provides evidence that you have paid the VRT.

Learn more about the VRT on the *revenue.ie*.

Motor Tax

The Irish Government imposes motor tax on all vehicles. Once your car has been registered, you will receive the Form RF100 Motor Tax Application which you will need to complete in order to pay the required motor tax. The motor tax on vehicles registered before July 2008 is determined by the CO_2 emissions. For vehicles registered after July 2008 the amount of motor tax that you will need to pay is dependent on the size of your vehicles engine.

You can pay your motor tax three, six, or 12 monthly, either online or at a Motor Tax Office. You will receive a motor tax disk to display on the windscreen of your vehicle. Renewal reminders will be sent to you.

Learn more about the motor tax at *motortax.ie*.

National Car Test (NCT)

The National Car Test (NCT) is required for all vehicles 4 years or older, regardless if the vehicle has undergone similar testing in other countries. The NCT assesses your vehicle for road worthiness e.g. brakes, rust, steering, emissions etc... The NCT needs to be carried out every two years, but for vehicles older than 10 years it will need to be carried out annually. If you do not get your vehicle tested as scheduled, you will face fines and penalty points.

Learn more about the NCT and to find your local testing centre at the *ncts.ie* website.

Motor Vehicle Insurance

You are legally required to have motor vehicle insurance when driving in Ireland. If you fail to do so, you may incur fines and penalty points and could be disqualified from driving.

Car Insurance Premiums

Car insurance premiums are determined by your:
- Age
- Gender
- Licence type – fully licensed drivers will get a better rate than provisional licence holders.
- Car type – older vehicles, expensive vehicles and high powered vehicles will be more expensive to insure.
- How frequently the vehicle is used – the more you use it, the higher the premium.
- Where the vehicle is kept – keeping your car in a secure garage will reduce your premium.

Insurance Types

Comprehensive Motor Vehicle Insurance

This is the highest level of cover, but consequently the most expensive. It typically covers you for all eventualities.

Third Party, Fire and Theft Motor Vehicle Insurance

This is mid-range insurance. It typically covers you for loss of your vehicle through fire or theft and damage to property. In addition, there are optional extras that you can take out such as windscreen breakage.

Third Party Motor Vehicle Insurance

This is the most basic form of insurance and is the minimum

cover that you must have by law. If you are at fault then only your passengers and the driver and passengers of the other vehicle/s are compensated. This type of insurance does not provide cover for your vehicle damage or if it is stolen or goes on fire.

Tips

- Always read the fine print and don't assume that all insurance policies will be the same.
- Shop around to find a good rate.
- Make use of comparison sites such as:
    - Chill *chill.ie*
    - Top Quote *topquote.ie*
    - Quote Me *quoteme.ie*
    - Paddy Compare *paddycompare.ie*
- Insuring a left-hand drive car can be difficult and expensive. If you are planning on bringing a left-hand drive vehicle into Ireland, then do the sums first to see if it is cost effective.

What to Do in an Accident

If you are involved in an accident, you must stop at the scene, no matter how extensive the damage is. Take the details of the other driver:

- Name
- Address
- Vehicle owner details (it may not be the owner of the vehicle that is driving at the time of the accident).
- Insurance details

If anyone is injured in the accident and/or there is property damage, you should report it to the Garda (police).

If you can, you should also take photographs of the scene of the accident and all damaged property (try to include the entire vehicle in case damage occurs after the accident and they attempt to attribute it to the accident). This can be submitted to the insurance company and Garda if necessary.

Tips

- The emergency number for the Garda and ambulance services is 112 or 999.

Vehicle Breakdown Services

Don't risk being stuck with a broken down vehicle in the middle of the Irish countryside. Get peace of mind by signing up for breakdown cover. If you are hiring a car, this service should be provided by the car hire company.

If you have comprehensive insurance, then breakdown service may be provided as part of your cover. However, the service that they provide may be limited, so check before joining any breakdown service.

The main Irish providers of breakdown services are:
- The AA *theaa.ie*
- Axa *axa.ie*
- Blue Insurance *blueinsurance.ie*
- Break Down Cover *breakdowncover.ie*
- Car Protect *carprotect.ie*
- Road Rescue *roadrescue.ie*

Importing a Car Into Ireland

Importing a car into Ireland can be very costly. Before doing so, make sure that you consider the costs.

If you are importing a car into Ireland, you must:
- Register the car.
- Pay VRT (if you can prove that you have owned the vehicle for 6 months or more, you won't be required to pay the VAT).
- Pay motor tax.
- Pay for vehicle insurances.

12 CULTURE

The Irish Language

The Irish language, known as 'Irish' when speaking in English or 'Gaeilge' if speaking in Irish, is originally a Celtic language. Many people mistakenly refer to it using the general term 'Gaelic', but Gaelic can refer to either the Scottish Gaelic language or the Irish Gaelic language, so you need to use the term 'Irish language'. However, if an Irish person is speaking to someone from another country, they may refer to it as 'Irish Gaelic', but only to try and make it clear what they mean.

Irish used to be the predominant language amongst the Irish, but its decline began during the English rule in the seventeenth century. The Irish language was further devastated during the Great Famine of 1845-52, where Ireland lost up to 25% of its population to emigration and death.

By the end of the British rule, less that 15% of the Irish population spoke the language. Since then Irish speakers have been a minority, but much effort has been made to preserve and promote the language. For example, it is taught in schools and there is also Irish speaking Radio and TV. Driving around Ireland, you will also see that most signs are bilingual and written in both Irish and English.

Although people speak English in Ireland, there are a number of regional communities where Irish is the main language spoken. These communities are collectively known as Gaeltacht or in plural as Gaeltachtaí. The Gaeltacht covers extensive parts of counties Donegal, Mayo, Galway and Kerry, parts of counties Cork, Meath and Waterford and six populated offshore islands.

I highly recommend that you take the time to travel to these Gaeltacht regions, as they are in some of Ireland's most beautiful areas. Try learning a few words in Irish so that you can connect with the locals.

Basic Irish Phrases

To get you started, here are some basic Irish phrases.
- Hello *Dia dhuit* (DEE-a GWIT) This translates as 'God be with you'.
- The response to this greeting is *Dia is Muire dhuit* (DEE-a iSS MWIRR-a Gwit) which translates as God and Mary be with you.
- How are you? *Conas atá tú?* (CUNN-us a-TAW too?)
- I'm well *Táim go maith* (TAW'm guh MAH).
- What is your name? *Cad is ainm duit?* (COD iss ANNim ditch?)
- My name is _____ is *ainm dom* (_____ iss annim dum)
- Nice to meet you *Deas ag bualadh leat* (JAHSS egg BOO-loo lyaht)
- Please *Le do thoil* (singular) / *Le bhur dtoil* (plural) (LE do HULL/LE wur DULL)
- Thank you/you (pl.) *Go raibh maith agat/agaibh* (GUH ROH MAH ug-ut/ug-iv)
- You're welcome (in response to 'thank you') *Go ndéanaí mhaith duit / daoibh* (singular / plural) (Goh nyae-nee why ditch / dee-iv)
- Yes *'Sea* (SHAA) *No Ní hea* (Nee haa) There is no exact translation for yes and no in Irish – these words mean 'it is'. People usually use the question verb again in their replies, in the positive or negative, in the same tense, voice and person as the question was asked.
- Excuse me *Gabh mo leithscéal* (Goh mah lesh-kyale)
- I'm sorry *Tá brón orm* (TAW BROHN urr-im)
- Goodbye *Slán* (Slawn)

- I can't speak Irish [well] *Níl Gaeilge [mhaith] agam* (neel GWAYL-geh [why] ug-um)
- Do you speak English? *An bhfuil Béarla agat?* (ahn will BAYR-la ug-ut?)
- Good morning *Maidin maith* (may-jin MY)
- Good evening *Tráthnóna maith* (Trah-no-nuh why)
- Good night *Oíche mhaith* (EE-hah why)
- I don't understand *Ní thuigim* (NEE HIGG-im)
- Where is the toilet? *Cá bhfuil an leithreas?* (CAW will ahn LEH-HER-as?)

Irish Language Resources

- Foras na Gaeilge is responsible for the promotion of the Irish language in Ireland. There is an English language option on the top right of their site *gaeilge.ie*.
- Want to know how to pronounce an Irish word or phrase? Then use *abair.tcd.ie*, a handy Irish language text to speech synthesis system which was developed by Trinity College.
- The Irish Dictionary which you can access online at *irishdictionary.ie*.

Free Online Introductory Irish Language Courses
- Raidió Teilifís Éireann (RTÉ) is the National Public Broadcaster for Ireland. On the *rte.ie* website they provide a FREE online Irish language course.
- There are a number of Irish language lesson series on YouTube.
- The Irish newspaper, the Irish Independent has published a collection of FREE MP3 and PDF Irish language resources on their website *independent.ie*.

Irish Language Forums

- The *irishlanguageforum.com* is a community site that provides Irish translation.
- Daltaí na Gaeilge promotes and teaches the Irish language. They also host an Irish language forum, and provide

resources and information about Irish language classes around the world on their website *daltai.com*.

Irish Language TV shows

- RTÉ the Irish National broadcaster has a TV channel TG4 that broadcasts TV shows in the Irish language, from news and current affairs to sports and drama.

Irish Language Radio Stations

There are a number of Irish language radio stations broadcast around Ireland. You can listen to them via your radio, TV, phone or computer. They also have podcasts.

- Raidió na Gaeltachta (RnaG) RTÉ the Irish National broadcaster has an Irish language radio station. Visit *rte.ie*.
- Anocht FM is a youth radio station that broadcasts between 9pm and 1am weekdays on the same frequency as RnaG. Visit *rte.ie*.
- Raidió Rí-Rá is growing in popularity and plays chart music for young people. Got to *rrr.ie*.
- Raidió na Life is a Dublin based Irish language radio station. There is an English language option on the top right of their website *raidionalife.ie*.

Irish Accents, Slang, Sayings and Nouns

Whilst travelling around Ireland, you will notice that the Irish accent varies a lot between regions, especially country versus city areas. This can be the butt of many jokes amongst the Irish people. (As I'm sure this also happens within your own country with varying dialects and accents).

There are thousands of slang words and sayings used in Ireland, so much so that there are whole websites devoted to it. As well as Irish wide terms, there are also many regional colloquialism. For a full list of Irish slang, visit the Irish Slang website *slang.ie*.

Some of my favourite ones that I have come across while living in Ireland are:

- *Acting the Maggot:* Fooling and messing around / behaving like a fool. You can refer to someone or something as

acting the maggot.
- *Craic:* Pronounced 'crack', it means what's happening / what's up / what's the gossip? e.g. "What's / how's the craic?".
- *Eejit:* A fool e.g. "He's an eejit".
- *Feck:* Although it sounds like the swear word 'fuck', it is a more socially acceptable version and is openly used in it's place e.g. "Feck it / Feck off".
- *Grand:* Used in place of good / fine / great e.g. "It'll be / that'll be grand".
- *Plastered:* Very drunk e.g. "I am / was plastered".
- *Puss:* Sulky face. "Take that puss of ya".
- *Shite:* Bad quality e.g. "It's a pile of shite".
- *Wrecked:* Tired – usually after a big night out e.g. "I'm wrecked".

What they don't say...

- *Top of the morning to you:* Despite popular belief by the outside world, the Irish do not use this saying. In fact they are quite tired of hearing this from tourists, so I recommend avoid mentioning it altogether!

Common Irish Nouns

Knowing some of the regularly used nouns will prevent you from looking so confused during a conversation:
- *Bulmers:* Irish cider, re-branded as 'Magners' abroad.
- *Croker:* Croke Park in Dublin (the main Irish sports stadium).
- *Football:* Soccer.
- *GAA:* Gaelic Athletics Association is the organisation responsible for Irish sport. Sometimes referred to as 'Gah' instead of the G.A.A.
- *Gaelic Football:* A type of Irish sport.
- *Handball:* A type of Irish sport.
- *Hot press:* The cupboard that the hot water heater the 'immersion' is kept in.
- *Hurling:* A type of Irish sport.

- *Immersion:* A type of water heating system commonly used in Ireland.
- *Jacks:* Toilet.
- *Minerals:* Soft drinks.
- *Petrol and Diesel:* Vehicle fuel (Americans gas). If hiring a car make sure you check whether it is petrol or diesel before filling it up.
- *Rounders:* A type of Irish sport.
- *Tayto:* Common Irish brand of crisps (chips).
- *The press:* Cupboard (don't get it confused with the 'hot press').

Irish Sports

The following Irish sports are governed by the Gaelic Athletic Association (GAA).

Tips

- Gaelic football and Hurling use the same type of field and goal.

Gaelic Football

Irish: *Peil Ghaelach*; short name *Peil* or *Caid*

Commonly referred to as *football* or *Gaelic*, Gaelic football is an Irish sport played between two teams of 15 players. Although considered a male only sport, a similar game of Gaelic football is played by women and it is regulated and promoted by the Ladies' Gaelic Football Association.

The rules are very similar to the Australian Rules football. It is played on a rectangular grass pitch with a goal post at each end. The goal post is like a combination of both the rugby and soccer goal posts. The ball is round and slightly smaller than a soccer ball.

You can hold the ball and run with it for a maximum of four steps, but if you want to run with it for any longer, then you either have to bounce it (but not twice in a row) or kick it back into your hands. Alternately, you can kick it along like a soccer ball. To pass the ball, you can either hit it with your hand or fist, or kick it.

There are two ways of scoring; you can shoot it over the goal posts for one point, or into the soccer like goal post net for three points. The opposition can try and block the ball with their hands or even barge you shoulder to shoulder. As can imagine, it's an exciting and fast moving game to watch.

Gaelic football is strictly an amateur sport, with players, coaches, and managers prohibited from receiving any form of payment. Although Gaelic football is mainly played on the island of Ireland, there are units of the Association that exist in other areas such as Great Britain and North America.

Tips

- To learn more about the rules and regulations of Gaelic football, visit the GAA Football website *gaa.ie*. For the women's Gaelic football, visit the Ladies Gaelic Football Club website *ladiesgaelic.ie*.

Hurling

Irish: *Iománaíocht / Iomáint*

Believed to be the world's oldest field game, Hurling is an Irish team sport played between two teams of 15 players, or 'hurlers'. It is governed by the Gaelic Athletic Association (GAA). Although considered a male only sport, a similar game called Camogie is played by women, and it is regulated and promoted by the Ladies' Gaelic Football Association.

It is played on a rectangular grass pitch with a goal post at each end. The goal post is like a combination of both rugby and soccer goal posts. Players carry a stick, or 'hurley'. It is similar to a hockey stick, but with a flatter wider curve at the end. The ball, or 'sliotar', is like a hockey ball but with raised ridges.

You can catch the ball in the sliotar with your hands and scoop it up with your hurley. You can move the sliotar up the field by kicking it, slapping it with an open palm, or hitting it with your hurley along the ground or into the air (a dangerous move for the players around them because they swing the hurley like a baseball bat!). Alternately, you can carry the sliotar in your hand for a maximum of four steps, or balance or bounce the sliotar on the hurley.

However you can't:

- Touch the sliotar on the ground with your hands.
- Throw the sliotar or hurley.
- Play the sliotar from your hand to the hurley more than twice in one possession.

You can use the hurley to block shots, make shoulder to shoulder contact with the person in possession of the sliotar, or the player nearest the sliotar.

There are two ways of scoring; you can either shoot it over the goal posts for one point, or into the soccer like goal post net for three points.

The hurlers wear helmets with a faceguard for protection, but they regularly suffer terrible hand injuries. My jeweller showed me a ring that was specially designed for hurlers. It opened with a hinge because many of them can't get a wedding ring over their permanently smashed knuckle.

Tips

- To learn more about the rules and regulations of Hurling, visit the GAA Hurling website *gaa.ie*. For the women's version of the game, Camogie, visit the Camogie website *camogie.ie*.

Gaelic Handball

Irish: *liathróid láimhe*

Known as Handball in Ireland, it's similar to the American handball. The basic rules of the game are to use your hand to strike the ball to make it hit the front wall and bounce twice before your opponent can return it.

In Ireland, they play four codes of handball. What differentiates these codes is the number of walls on the court, the size of the court, and type of ball that is used. It can be played as singles or doubles.

International Handball Codes

- **40×20** The most popular version 'Small Alley' uses a

40x20ft court enclosed with four walls. Players must wear gloves and eye guards as the small rubber ball used can reach speeds of up to 100mph. The season runs from November through to April.

- **One-Wall / Wall Ball** This code only uses one wall measuring 20x16ft, and can be played both indoor and outdoor. The season runs from May to August.

Traditional Irish Handball Codes

- **60×30 Softball** Referred to as 'Big Alley' or 'Softball', it's played on a 60x30ft court with a larger, bouncier ball. As a result, eye guards and gloves are not required. It is typically played in summer because it was traditionally played outside. The season runs from June to October.
- **60×30 Hardball** This code uses the same court size as Softball, but uses a small hard cork and leather ball. As it can travel over 100mph, eye guards and gloves are required. The season runs from May to June.

Tips

- To learn more about the rules and regulations of Handball, visit the GAA Handball website *gaahandball.ie*.

Rounders

Irish: *cluiche corr*

Rounders is a popular game amongst Irish school children and it is played at all age levels and also mixed teams. The game is a bat and ball game similar to baseball. It is generally believed that Baseball came from Rounders.

Rounders is played between two teams and there are five innings. One team fields, while the other bats, then they swap over after three outs. No more than nine players can be on the field at one time, but they can make up to three substitutes during play.

On the field are four bases. Points or 'rounders' are scored for each circuit that a batter makes without being made 'out'. Each batter gets three balls bowled to them. The bowler uses an underarm pendulum like motion to bowl. If the ball is considered badly bowled, then it is not counted as their three balls. If they get three bad balls then they can walk freely to the first base.

The batter is out if:

- On the third ball they don't hit it and the catcher (who stands behind them) catches the ball before it hits the ground.
- The bat gets thrown in a dangerous way or while running.
- On the third good ball they hit it into a foul area.
- They deliberately contact a fielder carrying the ball.
- They touch a base that has been 'tagged' by a fielder carrying the ball. However, the batter can try to go back to the previous base if it is not already occupied.
- If they try to occupy a base that is already taken by another batter (this excludes first base which they must vacate for the next batter).

Tips

- To learn more about the rules and regulations of Rounders, visit the GAA Rounders website *gaarounders.ie*.

Other Sports in Ireland

The Irish enjoy their sport. Golf is very popular and you will find a number of very good golf courses to enjoy. Horse riding is also popular. I recommend attending the annual Dublin Horse Show where you will find all forms of horse riding on display.

With people from all over the world living in Ireland, you can find a club for just about any sport. Joining a local sports team is a great way to meet new people and create new friendships.

Find a sporting club near you:

- Local Sports Clubs – Try the Golden Pages directory *goldenpages.ie*.
- *onlineclubmembers.com* – A hub for clubs.
- *yourlocal.ie* – A local directory.

Finding New Friends

Making new friends as an adult can be tough, and finding friends when you've relocated to a new country can be a daunting task. Making friends in your new workplace may be difficult. There is likely to be a much more diverse spread of ages in an office and they may already have their families and a wide social circle behind them.

Other than work, the best way to find new friends is to join a group of like minded individuals. However, the key is not just to attend the social events, but to then invite two or three people from it out for coffee or for a few drinks. Likewise, don't be afraid to accept invitations, no matter how daunting it seems.

Don't forget to ask people for contact details, and utilise social media and group messaging to help you to keep in touch with people. When you are establishing new friendships, you need to take the time and effort to maintain connections. It won't take long before you realize that these people are your new friends.

Participate in Sports and Fitness

Join a Sporting Team

Joining a local sports team is a great way to meet new people and create new friendships (as well as keeping fit of course). With people from all over the world living in Ireland, you can find a club for just about any kind of sport. Or you could consider trying your hand at traditional Irish sports like Gaelic football, hurling handball or rounders.

Find a sporting club near you:
- Local Sports Clubs – Use the Golden Pages directory *goldenpages.ie*.
- *onlineclubmembers.com* – A hub for clubs.
- *yourlocal.ie* – A local directory.

Join a Fitness Class

Whether it's Yoga, Pilates, Boxing or Aerobics, joining a regular class will provide you with the opportunity to meet new people, and hopefully develop friendships. Start by asking people out for a coffee after a class.

Join a Social Group

Spend some time on these websites to find a group or individuals with similar interests to meet up with.

meetup.com/cities/ie

The Meetup website provides lists of group meet-ups in cities across Ireland. Meetup aims to bring people with common interests together and to promote the development of local communities. Whatever your hobby or interest, there is sure to be a Meetup group for you where you can find other like minded people.

newtotown.ie

New to Town is a site for people looking to meet new people and make new friends in their area. On the website you will find listings by all kinds of individuals that are wanting to meet new people and develop friendships.

Sign up for a Night Course

Enrolling in a night course allows you to not only gain new skills, but also to meet new people and provide you opportunities to make new friends. Find a course that interests you at *nightcourses.com*.

Volunteer

Volunteering is a great way to not only meet new people, but also to become involved in and get to know your new community. Volunteer Ireland posts volunteer opportunities from all over Ireland on their website *volunteer.ie*, and also provides details about how to gain the volunteer position.

ABOUT THE AUTHOR

Originally from New Zealand, C L Mitchell lived in Australia for 10 years before moving to the Republic of Ireland with her husband in 2014. Using her knowledge and experience of moving to Ireland, C L Mitchell created the website *relocatingtoireland.com*, which provides practical information and advice to others planning on making the move.

In her spare time C L Mitchell loves to travel and experience new cultures, beliefs and foods. Her other passions include cooking, gardening, hiking and nature.

INDEX

A

Accommodation. *See* Housing
Airports, 8
Au Pair, 119–22, 131

B

Banking, 56–60
    choosing, 56
    irish banks, 57
    opening, 58
    opening hours, 57
    stamp duty charges, 59
    transferring funds, 59–60

C

Car ownership. *See* Vehicle ownership
Childcare, 129–31
Climate. *See* Weather
Coeliac, 5
Counties, 1
Currency, 2
Cycling, 159–61
    city bike scheme, 159–60
    cycle planner, 160–61

D

Disability, 4
Drinking laws, 5
Driver licensing, 169–76
    EU/EEA, 170
    exchange foreign licence, 170
    Irish licence, 172–76
    non EU/EEA, 170
    renting vehicle, 169
Driving, 163–80
    accidents, 165, 179
    breakdown services, 169, 180
    driver licensing, 169–76
    offences, 168
    road rules, 163–64
    roundabouts, 164–65
    safety regulations, 165
    toll roads, 167–68
    traffic reports, 169

    vehicle ownership, 176–80
    what to expect, 166–67

E

Education. *See* Schooling
Electricity, 84
Embassies and Consulates, 2
Emergency services, 2

F

Ferries, 8
Ferries to Ireland, 8
Flights to Ireland, 8
Friends. *See* Socialising

G

Garda. *See* Police
Gas, 84
Gluten intolerant, 5

H

Health insurance, 54–55
    lifetime community rating, 55
    regulations, 54
Health Service Executive, 44
Healthcare, 44–55
    children, 48
    emergency services, 47
    general practitioners, 46
    insurance, 54–55, 54–55
    long term illnesses, 48
    medical cards, 45
    medical tourism, 53
    medicines and pharmacies, 52–53
    private, 54–55
    public, 45–54
    sexual, 50, 52
    specialist services, 47
    women, 48–50
Heating, 68–72
    boilers, 69
    immersion, 71
    night storage, 69
    night storage water, 72
Higher Education, 136–39

Z

29250141R00114

Printed in Great Britain
by Amazon